WORLD PSALM

AMERICAN PSALM,

American Psalm, World Psalm

Nicholas Samaras

THE ASHLAND POETRY PRESS

Printed in the United States of America
ISBN: 978-0-912592-76-3

Library of Congress Control Number: 2013955803

Cover photo: Grisha Ressetar, Copyright 2001.

Typeface: Titles are set in Minion Pro, 20 point. Body text of poems is set in Perpetua, 12 point.

Cover design: Nicholas Fedorchak

Acknowledgements and References

Grateful recognition is given to these literary periodicals in which the following poems originally appeared:

Ancient Paths: "Psalm in the Words of a Simple Man to Emulate," "The Psalm of My Reality Now," "The Psalm of Useless Prayers," "Shiggaion"
Connotation Press: "Petition"
Image: "A Psalm to Say These Words Until I Can Hear Them," "A Psalm to the Mansions of Heaven," "Psalm as Frustration I Can Live With," "The Psalm of Then," "The Psalm of Your Face," "Sacred Air," "The Unpronounceable Psalm"
In Touch Magazine: "Offering the Vast and the Mere," "Psalm of Waking"
The Literary Review: "Psalm for the Song and the Singing"
The Penwood Review: "A Christian Psalm"
Relief: "A Lighter Vessel," "The Alone of My Time," "Considering the Nature of God"
Sojourners: "Lent"
The Southern Review: "Benediction," "Contemplating the Nature of Hell," "Everything in Existence Is Dialogue"
World Literature Today: "Rebetiko Psalm"

"Benediction" was anthologized in *Before the Door of God*. Editors, Hopler, Jay and Kimberly Johnson; New Haven: Yale University Press (2013): 360.

"Benediction," Contemplating the Nature of Hell," and "The Psalm of Then" were reprinted in *Ancient Paths*. Issue 16. Virginia (January, 2011): 8-20.

"The Psalm of Then," along with being featured on multiple Internet Websites and blogs, was reprinted in the *Mennonite Brethren Herald*. Winnipeg, Manitoba, Canada (April, 2009): 2.

Unless individual poems are in strict (and obvious) stanzaic form, there are no strophe breaks from one page to the next of any poem of multiple pages.

"Psalm Defined" contains an image inspired by and paraphrased from the late American composer, philosopher, social critic, conceptual artist, film director, score composer, deconstructionist, and ideologue of modern classicism, Frank Vincent Zappa.

"Sacred Air" was written after my conversation with the visual artist, Michael Sitaras, who was assembling a conceptual art exhibit by bottling air from sacred sites over the earth and exhibiting the "filled" bottles, with even the bottles themselves becoming exquisite modes and statements of artistic expression and commentaries on their place of origin.

❖

Asaph:	A convener, or collector; a Levite; one of the leaders of David's choir; someone skilled in music, and a "seer." The "sons of Asaph" were King David's descendants, or more probably a class of poets or singers who recognized him as their master.
Ashan:	In Hebrew, the word for "smoke."
Athos:	"Mount Athos," the Holy Mountain, a geographical place of spiritual pilgrimage located in northeastern Greece on a peninsula of densely-forested land. While Christians have retreated there since the first century, the first systematically-organized Christian monastery was established there in the tenth century.
Baǧlama:	A type of stringed musical instrument shared by various cultures throughout the Eastern Mediterranean, Near East, and Central Asia. In the blues music of Greece, the name *Baǧlama* is given to a treble *bouzouki*, a closely-related instrument.
Canboulay:	Island Carnivals emerged from French Colonist Masters. Because the native and imported slaves were not allowed to participate in any Carnival, they managed to form their own celebration, called the Canboulay.
Cariso:	A Trinidadian word that refers to "old-time" Calypso songs. Deriving from "Cariso," the word "calypso" emerged into prominence in the 1930s and grew dominant when European colonists began printing the word. Most famously featured in Homer's *The Odyssey*, the original Calypso was an enchantress who, through her song, captivated Odysseus for seven years.
Gittith:	A Biblical, stringed instrument of music.

Guf: In Jewish mysticism, the Chamber of Guf (also Guph or even Gup), Hebrew for "body," also called the *Otzar* (Hebrew for "treasury"), is the Treasury of Souls, located in the Seventh Heaven.

Hesychast: One who practices the Eastern Orthodox concept of Hesychasm, the art of developing internal stillness. Hesychasm comes from the Greek word "isychia," meaning quietness or tranquility.

Hoda'ah: In Hebrew, the word for "thanks" or "gratitude."

Kaiso: The root word of *cariso* or *calypso* is "kaiso," meaning "continue" or "go on, go on."

Lafayette
Park: In the American Capitol of Washington, D.C., the park area in front of the White House, in which people are allowed to congregate for organized protesting of political issues.

Leipsana: Holy relics of a saint, usually a body part or an article of clothing worn by the saint.

Maskil: Someone who is wise, prudent; a maskil is also an instruction.

Miktam: A Miktam is, to me, the most fascinating subgenre of psalms and element of a psalm. The meaning of the term is disputed. A Miktam is either an engraving, a permanent writing, something made of gold, a special teaching, or something hidden. Other suggestions include a musical notation or a title for psalms connected with the expiation of sin. I myself greatly prefer the understanding of a Miktam as a hidden story. For example, students of the Biblical Psalms believe there is a story hidden within the 60th Psalm.

Rebetes: In the Greek language, the term for "Singers of the Blues."

Sheminith: A musical term, supposed to denote the lowest note sung by men's voices. Or an eighth mode, a divisional order in processions.

Shiggaion: From the verb *shagah*, "to reel about through drink." The word denotes a lyrical poem composed under strong mental emotion; a song of impassioned imagination accompanied with suitable music: a dithyrambic ode. An alternate interpretation is from the verb *sha'ag*, "to cry aloud."

Skoufo: A small, round, informal and simple black-cloth head-covering often worn by monastics.

❖

Always, I thank the editors and teachers who encouraged my work, among them Joseph Brodsky, Kurt Brown and Laure-Anne Bosselaar, Stephen Dunn, Jonathan Galassi, Jorie Graham, Daniel Halpern, Stanley Kunitz, Cameron Lawrence, Robert Lowell, Anne Sexton, Daniel Simon, Mark Strand, Derek

Walcott, and Philip Zaleski; and my friends, among them Debra Bruce, Cyrus Cassells, Constance Donovan, Li-Young Lee, Heather Sellers, and Gerald Stern. And to Dr. John Kazes and June Kazes. I'm especially grateful to Gregory Wolfe, editor of the journal *Image*, and director of The Glen Institute, for his encouragement and support.

I thank the editors of the Ashland Poetry Press, Stephen Haven and Sarah Wells, for their kind professionalism and input.

I thank those who shared their spiritual and editorial insights in my writing of this book: David Harrity, Gus Hartofilis, Dean Kostos, Anastasios Kozaitis, and John Nieves.

I thank Steven Rubin who, through the Suncoast Writers Conference of the University of South Florida, informally commissioned me to write a benediction for each annual dinner evening. Over five years, these dinner benedictions turned into five psalms in the fourth Book of Gratitude.

I express my deepest gratitude to my father, Reverend Father Kallistos Samaras, for whom everything I write is dedicated, who raised me in the music and language of his sermons, in the cadence of his breathing, his joy and humour, in the strength of his devotion, in emotional stability, and the peaceful stillness of our family together.

I remember and thank Michael and Anna Cantonis.

Gratitude to Metropolitan Nikitas Lulias for the depth of his spiritual discussions and insights, and for his friendship and encouragement; always to Joni Mitchell, who taught me the colors of words; to Ian Anderson, Paul McCartney, Pete Townshend, Paul Simon, Gil-Scott Heron and The Last Poets for teaching me the structures of songwriting, and for all the singers of the Blues, who gave us the voices of our souls.

I began this writing because I always perceived the Biblical Psalms to be pure songs, as the most powerful of rhythms and choruses. From my father, in my childhood, I learned the etymology of the word "psalm" derived from the Greek root, "psalmós," meaning a song sung to the accompaniment of music, and how the antiphonal structures of psalms allowed for call and response, a dialogue in refrain, petition, and answer. For me, music was always built into the very word psalm. As a teenager, I referred to the Psalms as the "top forty" of the year 500 B.C.

I consider myself to be a political writer, a social commentator. I have always enjoyed the humour of Steven Wright who observed that it's been two thousand years since the Biblical New Testament was composed; he felt the Bible should now be referred to as "the Old Testament and the Most Recent Testament." From that truth in humour, I enjoyed imagining how the psalms might be rendered in contemporary times, filtered through the soulful structures of American music, in blues form, jazz form, folk, modern pop, and hip-hop form, in cadences and structures of contemporary World music throughout all countries, musical refrains that carried us through the centuries, how a modern soul could wail its heart, and what universal resonance would remain. Even if modern styles of music, popular for their time, might fade and vanish, the lyrics and their literary devices would still remain. I view it an excellent approach to think of contemporary psalms in terms of the experimental nature of modal Jazz—the arrangement extending outward in improvisation, but always returning to its base form. In this, I regarded the extension of imagined modern psalms as likewise extending outward—yet always returning to the Biblical Psalms in measure of base structure, theme, content, literary device, and lyrical expression, illuminating what may be constant in human struggle—social, political, and artistic.

Every form of artistry (including prayer) begins in rhythm, cadence, music, and relationship. In the words of David Essex, "Rock on, ooh, my soul."

—*Nick Samaras*

Contents

Book II

Petition the Lord

Book III

Movement

Book IV
Gratitude, the Father of Praise & Humility

Book V
Stillness

Again and always—

For, and because of,
KALLISTOS GEORGE SAMARAS,
my father

Book I

Breath

Origin

Of course, there were things
that didn't make it into books.

Presence uncontained.
Gesture understood.

Individual stories
that were one story, ongoing.

For a time, trees were safe
from the miller and the mill.

Journals were lived, endings
not reached.

Language was born
when the first angels fell.

The Unpronounceable Psalm

I couldn't wrap my mouth around the vowel of your name.
Your name, a cave of blue wind that burrows and delves
endlessly, that rings off the walls of my drumming, lilting heart,
through the tiny pulsations of my wrists, the blood in my neck.
I couldn't hold the energy of your name in my mouth
that was like trying to utter the crackle of lightning,
as if my teeth would break from its pronunciation.
I am dwarfed in the face of your magnitude,
O you whom I can't articulate. O you of fluency
and eloquence whom I can't fully express, my words
are only the echo of you that rings within my soul, my soul
a cave of blue wind that houses the draft of you,
the eternal vowel of you I can't wrap my mouth around.
Lord, Lord, as close as I may gather, as close as I may say.

The Psalm of Nothing

Lord, I start with nothing.

I start with only your spark on my breath,
the exhalation of feeble desire.

I start with nothing.

I first meet the Lord as my creator.
I live in the center.
I emanate when I breathe.
I speak with my breath.
What I exhale, I bring
back within.

Without the Lord, I remain
nothing in my own devices.
I become a grown man
without purpose, without relation or identity.
There is nothing real without identity and relation.

Even the monk holds relation with his prayer.
Even the hermit holds
dialogue with his heartbeat.

Lord, my feeble song is this human need
to write it down and make it real.

Even a grown man may breathe out a prayer.
Even a grown man may remain a child inside.

As a child, I thought a man's chest
was invincible. I marveled at my father's

massive chest and mane, his Alexandrian breathing.

Now grown, I question everything of myself.
My own lion chest becomes no shield
but the thing, one day, to betray my breath.

Now mature enough to pray, I say,
Lord, let me speak with my breath
while I have breath.
Let me come from healing and go to healing.
Lord, soften my calloused heart.

Let me venerate my start
by hallowing the passage of my ending.

I was brought from
nothing into something—
a soul, a spark to honor
the breath of my father.

Mature now to know I have not been the center.
Mature now to know how to cleanse by breathing.
Aspire the Lord and exhale myself.
Aspire the Lord and exhale myself.

Psalm Defined

In a drawing room of candlelight,
the tiny hearts of flames and wicks

flickered in response
to sound waves coming

from recorded music.
Music, a recipe for sculpted air.

And people's souls became
drawn into that room,

gathered to voice
by the melody and visual breath,

the light and movement, the physical presence—
attentive.

Corporate

A Psalm in Antiphony

Why are we here in the house of darkness and the house of light?
We come together to give more light to darkness.

What are you doing?
I am breathing.

What are you giving?
I am giving breath.

What am I to this giving?
You are giving back.

In the Valley of Salt

A Miktam of rescue from the underground
and adoption for the sons of the Lord

When we were born in the wrong place,
the Lord called us out to rectify circumstance.
When we were pulled to the wrong space,
the Lord moved the earth and the days.

We rode the engine underground
and the village of Hellein consumed us.
We slid down into the cool earth to lick
the cavern walls of salt and be nourished.

Oh, the green hills above us were good.
We sailed on a subterranean lake, the cold water
splashed on our trailing fingers and hands,
the seasoned light guiding us upward.

When we were born in the wrong place,
kidnapped by chance, the Lord looked on in silence
until he brought us to safety. And we broke
into gold sunlight, breathless runaways to the Lord,

necromanced into living again. Led to the right parent
at the altars of Quincy, we claimed the quiet
cities of the Lord, in the valleys of salt,
in the safe places illumined by sodium light.

Byzantine Icon in the Saint Nicholas Chapel, Flushing, New York

Ἡ Χῶρα τοῦ Ἀχωρήτου

How may paint depict the world,
the universe and all it contains?

In gold and red gilt, a woman gestures
forward, the felt of her garment folding

in, the child in her lap looking
outward to us.

How we receive all time and all space,
the contours of the cosmos in a human face,

in the country of the ungraspable,
the container of the uncontainable.

Offering the Vast and the Mere

Address of the Heavens,
celestial Father, Creator,

I have reviewed my whole life,
every moment and praise,

every mistake and amnesia.
All I can offer is the totality

of my longish life in gratitude to you.
All I can offer is the totality of myself,

without the mereness of words,
to you who are

beyond words and silence,
who are beyond summation,

further than description.
All language to you is mere.

I am every human language
that fails to fully express.

All I can offer is my soul,
cleansed of myself in death,

cleansed of my willful ignorance
by your breathless compassion and mercy.

All I can offer—my breath
singing over my vocal chords.

All I can offer—my breath and vision
upon this ordinary page.

‏ne Psalm of Not

Not breath, but breathing.
Not me, but Christ in me.
Not me, but the Holy Spirit in me.

Not breath, but breathing.
Not justification, but repentance.
Not me, but my neighbor first.

Not time given, but time used.
Not my chance, but my helping
others find their chance.

Not breath, but breathing.
Not a prayer based on need or fear,
but a prayer based on love.

Not the act, but the action.
Not me, but the ancestors comprising me.
Not my hands, but the craft of my hands.

Not me, but my daughter and my son.
Not me, but my father in me, glimmering.
Not breath, but breathing.

Psalm of the Constant Day

For you are our God . . . forever existing, forever the same.
—from one of the (inaudible) prayers
in Saint John Chrysostom's Divine Liturgy

Then, what can be forever the same
for us through endless history?

Each young man will pine for love.
Every young girl will wait for any promise.

War has so many aliases, we are numb by them.
But it's the same name.

Generations exhale the equivalent prayers.
The unchanging Lord breathes His unchanging sigh.

We age through the same passions, same urgencies.
Only the toys change.

Everybody lives in modern times.

A Psalm to Say These Words Until I Can Hear Them

I will my soul to wake, and my soul does not wake.
My mind busies with itself, remembering
forgotten songs from my adolescence.
My mind recalls anything, so as not to listen.
Lord, I will my hands to be calm
and they fly to my teeth to crease my nails.
Lord, I will myself to be still
so I can hear the tiny voices in me,
screaming *look at me, look at me* . . . .
I will myself to be still so I can embrace the world
but there is too much of the world inside already.
Lord, I ask you to enter me and live here
but the clutter and noise evict you.
Lord, I am sick of myself.
I am no longer funny or entertaining or clever.
Lord, I will myself to cease.
I will myself to focus a breath apart, a breath
not held or stuttered but deepened.
I will myself to step aside. I will my soul to wake
and, though I do not wake, I am stirring.

The Psalm of Breath and Breathing

Sometimes, I become aware I'm holding my breath.
I breathe like a broken bellows. The day starts

and stutters. Mindless, I hold my breath in concentration,
in frustration, the old disruptive habits of holding, tightening,

the momentary ceasing and fear of stopping, the punching
out and the struggle back in. Then, what is the structure of breath

and how do we live with this difficult creature in our chests?
Every breath in is gratitude. Every breath out is fear.

The spine gathers on the inhale and lengthens on the exhale.
Breath is the servant to what happens. Breath maps the body

and, when I can allow it, I feel the release:
the deepening of breath into prayer, the deepening

of the body into creation. How is this paradox
of coming closer with expansion, the clarity of distance,

the breathing toward? I support the breath in singing. I fight
inhibiting emotion, impulse, expression, movement.

My posture is attitude, my breathing attitude. We become
the shape of our habits and the shape of our breathing.

We become the shape of our prayer lives, to resist
the behavior of tightening, holding. Every breath in

is gratitude. Every breath out is fear.
Deep and regular, prayer is the breath

of ocean sounding. Give me the prayer of a cleansing breath
and a focal point. Allow me the breath that combines

air and fire. Let me breathe clear to my soles.
Every breath in, gratitude. Each breath out, fear.

I breathe out the world. I breathe in the Lord.
All I am is the breath of faith that allows this dust to walk.

Presence

The sound of the house when the house is asleep.
The long space at the foot of the bed, at four a.m.

The framed photographs rectangled on the walls,
onlooking cubes of darkness in the darkness.

You come to me in moonlight.
You come to me as moonlight.

You come to me as the very
breath in my body.

You come to me.

Offertory

When we think of breath,
remember breath is spirit.

When we think of spirit,
remember spirit

is the presence of the Lord within us.
Then, in presence,

give breath
to our witness,

the spirit of our songs which are
our lives in creation.

Psalm of the Exasperated Lord

Why these hands? Why this countenance?
You speak for the dying in Constantinople.
Though your same prayers make even me wince,
still I hold your breaths as ruby and opal.

Then, why these hands and countenance?
All extinction returns to life in me.
I hold the dying now, the dying since.
I go by motive, but you go by degree.

Then, why these hands and this countenance?
You talk through your prayers, fleeting as birds.
I speak in your stillness so you may advance.
I listen more to the spaces between your words.

Put on sackcloth and lose your body.
Put on ash and taste the earth.
Each breath in is delay. Each breath out is hurry.
There is a weight to experience. There is a girth.

Then, why these hands and why this countenance?
Put on humility to lay in your bed.
Put up your soul to pray for the dying.
Put on these glasses and see the dead.

Psalm of Anointing

Lord, who will speak for the world?
The embodied houses we rest our souls in.
The material realm we breathe through.

Who will stand for the lame and the slanted,
the dropped and the upheld?
I will write for the world.

I will be a blues refrain if it soothes our burden,
say it twice for a feeling to be believed
more deeply. Some artists may reach high

but they don't reach us,
have the ability but no anointing.
When I think in poetry, I feel God's pleasure.

When I think of creation, I give my hobbled dancing.
We sing for the world as clear as we can.
Blues men keep everything poignant in focus.

Everything between God and humanity is metaphor.
Since all we can write about are moments,
I write to rescue.

Now, every page, canvas, and song
is an ode. Every refrain is communion
in the holy sacrament of my pen.

Rebetiko Psalm

Then, sing a psalm of the outsider race—
an entire nation of us without borders,
a conglomerate tribe of exiles recognisable

by the same light in our same eyes.
We were Anatolian and Greek under the Ottoman boot.
We were African and immigrant processed

over the waves of the flat, gray Atlantic.
We came from mainlands possessed by others.
Once native, we were suddenly ethnic.

We came from Alatsata, thrown out of our homes
and our country. Everyone was the Lord's people—
but we were still cast off from even our Holy Altars, thrown

into the dust of the roads leading
out of every town, disinterred from even
the cemeteries of our ancestors—

evicted from the dust of the world
and plunged into the coldest harbors across the seas—
not even our own abroad wanting us—but repelling us

on from the pocked ports of Bodrum, Piraeus,
Liverpool, and Ellis Island, funneling to the factories of Woburn.
And in exile, what did we ever find but ourselves,

a stark room to decorate—the wind
chugging into our scarves, our rolled-up coats for pillows,
the damp wool souring our breath?

We became alienation and exile from everything we'd known.
We left behind the bones of our ancestors in graves
only the wind would comb.

We were emptied eyes and haunted souls
who established shanty towns outside of Athens, who sifted
into new ghettos of the Mani. What could we do

but become the other of ourselves, until we were irreducible?
What could we do but sing into the wind and darkness,
to cup the breeze of our leaving?

We were blues before blues. We were exile and alienation
until the blues were always with us, until
we couldn't remember a generation or place or time

without blues. We became *Rebetes* who sang and played
for all the suffering and lost, played for survival and all
the rag-alley years of missing homes and homeland.

In this way, we lived through transit, subsisted through
the squabbled and claimed neighborhoods of the world.
We lived through countries. We existed through dictatorships.

We endured through emigration and deportation.
The word was refugee, with no countries wanting us.
Our resting was brief—our homes became transit until

we were citizens of transience. Even the wind, empty of us.
So, we filled our emptiness. We were ordinary souls,
some turning to the narcotic of sorrow for loss and misfortune,

some turning to the melodies of the melancholic and crooning——
a spliff of amnesia and a dancing for sorrow.
We tied up with the bağlama. Our daily living became the minor

chords of the gittith. Rootless, we became a roots music,
full of grief and passion, romance and bitterness.
When our lives became a haze of coastal cities and alleys,

the cradles of the tavern and the den became our hearth.
The prison and the boarding house became our nests.
When all we could hold was our breaths——

we breathed *Alatsata*. We breathed *ancestors.*
Our breathing accompanied castanets and clattering glass,
the droning of worry beads tapped against a sweating drink.

We sang of Smyrna and Pontos. We sang and the songs
possessed us, so we could possess something——
a life, an identity held in our breaths, individuals held together.

We sang for generations, citizens in nameless countries until
we became our own country of song. Singing our breaths, we moved
into ourselves——singing our breaths to make sure we're alive,

we were a universal tribe cast into the universe,
singing to be still, a soulful psalm of an outsider
nation singing to belong, to be home.

When One Has Suffered by Breathing

On the Cross, he couldn't breathe.
The wounded healer.

On the Cross, the universe
slid from his knifed ribs.

What is unassumed is unhealed—why

Christ had to become us completely,
assuming us to heal us.

True sacrifice is not giving what we have
but giving what we are.

Then, what do we do with our suffering?
Make it not any passive suffering,

but take it up, carry it
and carry through.

Do it daily, and constantly renew
ourselves to the Lord.

The Resurrection is inseparable from the Crucifixion.
Assume our waning bodies, then.

Gather our various pains
and hobble onward to our own harrowing.

Psalm of a Community

By myself, I am a failure.
With my father, I am the greatest son on earth.

By myself, I am a failure.
With my children, I am gentle and thinking of others.

By myself, I am a failure.
With the Lord, I am a child again
wanting to please a parent, wanting
to be good for the sake of goodness.

By myself, I am a failure.
But with the world, I am a person
struggling, a part participating in success.

By myself, I am a personal failure.
But I don't forget to pray for others,
for others live in my world, as well.
I am not separate unto the Lord.

By myself, I am a failure
if I am not attentive to the needs
of those who have so little in life.

By myself, I am a failure
if I ever think I am by myself.

For the Lord hears my thoughts,
for the Lord is a dialogue,
even as I'm alone with prayer,
with green wind in the trees,
with this breathing life.
What is failure in that?

Psalm of the Quietest Wailing

I.

It is attention that makes worship.

II.
I came to the rubble of history
to notice.

I walked up to the last wall
and touched the stones yellow with history.

I could only whisper into the crevices,
their centuries softened.

Not a shred of paper, but only
my breath as a scrap of witness.

Only my breath saying
I have come back, I am here with you.

III.

There was something I wanted to contain within myself.

There was something I wanted to let go.

IV.

What is justice but an acknowledgement of dignity?
What is virtue but whispering, *Who am I?*

V.

Leaving the place, I rode back to my life.

Now, when walls breathe in rooms, I pay attention.

VI.

In my solitude, the writing from my hands is the quietest wailing,
the witness of breath against a listening wall.

VII.
When wind carries in from far fields and absent cities,
I can hear a voice whispering in a wilderness.

Vaguely, it sounds like mine.

The Psalm of Your Face

Lord, let your face be lined.
Lord, let your hair be gray with patience.
Holy Father, let your cheeks be silver with long growth
as you put up with me and put up with me.
Lord, let your face be a blazon of parts
in which I can name you sufficient
to be seen in your unseen presence.
Lord, let your face be lined
with the knowledge of my sins.
Let your brow be uncreased in forgiveness.
Lord, let your eyes be clear of lightning
and your foggy voice unbass itself of thunder.
Lord, let your face be lined
and your massive chest be peaceful in breathing,
the falling and rising that is my slow way to you.

Sacred Air

Speak to me
about the presence of absence.

Not everything created
can be seen.

As the uncreated
may be glimpsed from a slant.

What we bring is attention—
prayer in our hands, spirit in our lungs.

Emptiness—but a focus on what
borders and frames the space—

what the space is filled by.
Nothing empty

of the presence of the Lord.
Give pause between words.

A container saying,
Don't look at me, but look

at the space of me. Look through me
to what I contain. A bottle filled

with the air of a holy place,
a desert, a mountain, a space

of the Lord to apprehend and inhabit.
Breathe the sacred air.

Psalm of the Smallest Annunciation

Father, what words do I ever own?
What words may I possess enough
to give back to you? All I may say
of myself is: Lord, I am here.

Others have said the same to you
and, though I am no prophet,
no saint, no chosen, I say it still:
Here I am, Lord. I am here.

Covered in a breathing darkness,
I am here and calling back to you.
Covered in my sinful self, I am here.
Diminished as I am by sin, here

I am, despite myself, I am here—
take me in my small annunciation,
in the breathing of my darkness,
in the fane of my folded hands.

The Nature of Giving

What was given to me, I am compelled
to give back. Father, I become the son
gazing back to my origin:

that my breath bespeaks breath,
that my gaze denotes vision,
that my hands reach out to feel

the tangible, the gold and red flecks
of depiction in a holy icon, their
burnished faces and eyes gazing

back out to me in connection.
Lord, how the Divine Liturgy
is called "the sensuous liturgy,"

in that I mark myself in the compass of the Cross,
my hands grasp the wafting smoke of incense
rising with the wisps of my prayer, my ears

cup the refrains of harmony hymned,
that I taste Christ's communion, melting
in its goodness and its reality.

Father in my hands, Father in my beating
heart and soul, I become the son, both
errant and not errant, both conscious

and subconscious. I become the son
who recognizes enough to know
I've actually been given

so much I'm as impelled
as my breathing to lift my hands
and offer all of it back.

Psalm of Uncreation

Lord, the length of your patience
is the braid of my living that binds me,
until even the gazing on you makes and unmakes me.

What was I before you? Who am I with you, but yours—
still myself but myself in you? My breath is unstrung
until all I can wish for is made from you.

Father, I was born wrong so birth me again.
Let the bad seed be uprooted and replaced.
I pray to be uncreated, and created anew.

Singing from my center of being, I yearn to be
disassembled, restrung. Let me be unwoven
and made in a new weave. Let the braid of me

be wound from you and wound from you
until I am strong with your plait.
Whole in your part, I am my definition in you.

Uncreate me to what I never was.
Ravel me. Unravel me. Entwine me back again.
My name in yours. My name in you.

Psalm of Belief and Unbelief

Lord, although I know you are there,
let me know you are there.

Lord, I know you are with me
but be with me.

I know you hear my every breath
but hear me, Lord.

I am the draft at the insulated window,
the lingering child in the adult.

I am the light overcome by night,
the persistent wavering that calls out,

Lord, although I know you are there,
let me know you are there.

As I know you are with me, be with me
while I overcome myself, Lord—and hear

my every breath.

New Century Confession

Inside the Lord, I am outside Time.
Inside my heart, I feel the presence
of the Holy Trinity: what it means

to feel the absolute certainty of blessing.
Alone, I am a dialogue in dialogue
with the Father, the Son, our Spirit.

There the touch of grace—with only
for me to open my heart to feel.
What is there but Love? What is there

but for me to open to the fact?
If I stop my every distraction and breathe,
I may feel the grace that lifts me, at last.

When my mind may grow finally still,
what is there for me but to recognize?
What is there for me but to rise?

Alone, there is no alone. Alone,
I am intimate with my breath
that is the Lord's inbreathing.

Alone, I say Lord, I say Jesus Christ
and the descent of the one Spirit.
Alone, I may feel the final absolute.

This elemental alone—irreducible—empiric—
I am a trinity of holiness touched. Alone,
I confess a trinity given to me and given

back. Alone, I am this incarnate soul reaching
out whose word is living consecration,
whose first nature and final name is love.

Book II

Petition the Lord

A Psalm to the Mansions of Heaven

Where the Lord lives in Heaven, is he lonely?
Does our Father walk his marble floors without
the company of anyone righteous? Who alone
is venerable enough to keep the Lord company?

My voice is small, yet I call to your house, Lord.
Does the wind enter your chambers and rooms,
cold and empty? Where are the souls of the righteous,
and how may they warm you? I call to your house.

Lord, I look for you in every neighborhood.
I knock on the doors of your churches and splinter
my knuckles to find my home in you. Who alone
is venerable enough to keep the Lord company?

The breezes of seraphic wings call for speech.
The chorus of saints harmonize in hazed light.
The harrowed, holy families lay their repentence
before the thrones of Christ and the Twelve Apostles.

May they live well and reach down to us living
who are sublet and mortgaged, deeded, indebted.
Lord, I also bring repentance to offer for earnest money.
Even in this life, I ask to sit in your drafty parish home.

I'd be satisfied to live in a shack on the back roads
of Heaven, just to live closer to you and visit, sometimes.
What I learned in the exotic air and streets of Jerusalem
is that, without company, even Paradise is lonely.

Lament Before the Lord

Lord, why are even your saints silent to me?
And my own patron saint who has never
appeared to me to my knowledge.

Lord, I call into the mouth of a cave,
my cries ringing through diminishing air,
going lighter and slighter as they fall.

What are the conditions of my living?
We are in eternal search for meaning.
Then, what am I without relation?

Oh, Father in Heaven, I have always
been on the outside of every group,
always on the outside.

Never a measure of acceptance.
My scars have run deep and hard.
Lord, this world is a cancer ward.

Still, I cry—Lord, soften my calloused heart.
Then, I will move from lamentation. I won't
have it any longer. I won't curse. I will

never curse, but I will look
everywhere for the visible works of the Lord
to hold me to faith. Say what you will

in this terminal ward
or hold silence in your mouth,
as the saints hold to it, patient and waiting.

Be sound or caesura.
Circumstances balance strangely.
We're not fair to God, either.

A Psalm of Grief

Who else can I call on but the Lord
in this world of deafness and blindness?
To whom else can I honestly express
how much I grieve for those who confuse
religion with culture, who worship
culture and socialize religion.

I grieve for humble voices drowned
out, made mute, and anything righteous
turned to look eccentric or fanatic.
Who else can I call on but the Lord
in this world to soften the heart that mourns,
the heart that breaks for a broken world?

I will make the distinction between religion and culture.
I will sing a psalm of grief for tears
to soften the stones of the world,
a lament to make palpable
the hearts of people who confuse
culture with worship and worship with nothing.

Though the world breaks me,
I refuse to crumble from the hard grief,
yet who else can I call out to, Lord,
against unpopular faith, against blind vision and deaf ears?
Who else can soften the heart and give value to stones
but the Lord of grief, the Lord of tears?

Psalm Unto Daydreaming

Lord, what prevents me from the Lord
but myself? The daydreaming that is cute
as a child is less welcome as an adult.

I become the grown dreamer,
impractical, unhelpful, all attention
to nothing but attention deficit.

I become the unfocused, the undisciplined.
I remain the incessant music of my adolescence,
the white noise that holds me from myself,

holds me from facing anything of myself.
I daydream during the Divine Liturgy.
I half-hear anything said to me in earnestness.

I become the endemic icon of our time.
Ours is now a century of compression.
We can't sustain prolonged attention.

We can't sustain the slow accrual
of reading one hundred and fifty psalms.
I pray, but look—how pretty these clouds.

Today, paying attention takes too long.
Nowadays, instant gratification takes too long.
Still, of all things, I'm impatient

with myself. Bring me back to you
and the thought of you.
Father in Heaven, hold me to you.

I am sorry for my uncontrolled fantasies.
I am sorry for my selfish prayers.
Forgive the music in the back of my head

that drowns out my best intentions,
my focus and my scant attention.
Forgive these ever-present

sound worms that burrow through my brain,
when I try to focus on the Lord.
Lord, there is no room for a dreamer,

no room for a poet or visionary.
I am dross to time. I am no substance.
Even I realize it is finally and daily time

to come to repentance. I come to repentance.
Hold me fast in your attention
and don't let my attention wander.

Let me live in magnification—
my heart that wants to be sincere,
paying attention and paying attention again.

e Psalm of Useless Prayers

To become holy.

To become a philanthropist by winning the lottery.

To make someone love me.

To make me taller and handsome.

To change everyone else.

To understand the opposite sex.

To have my children do what I wish.

To keep my hair.

To ask for things apart from good health.

To write my speech for the Nobel committee.

To have a Church without conflict.

To bargain for anything.

To fit in the clothes I wore when seventeen.

To go back and live in a time of innocence.

To live my life without fantasy—
       which is fantasy.

To not pay the cost of time on these prayers.

To have the fleeting time back.

Sometimes, Change Is a Longer Night

On what nights do I sing a dark psalm?
I would give up everything for the Lord
yet some things hold me strongly
since my youth. Since my youth,

I have dreamt of dark women
from the Mediterranean, women from the Islands,
smoky-voiced, rivers of raven hair
wafted by Sirocco winds, Moroccan breezes.

You can't petition the Lord with prayer
if you don't really care to make the change.
Yet the Greek word for repentance—*metanoia*—
literally means "I change my mind."

And the mind, truly the last to change.
I dream of dark women who come
from the curves of the Aegean.
I pine for Indian women in the cleavage

of night, the moon rising in irradiated fever.
Years now into marriage, even my aging
still appreciates the flower of dark beauty,
contemplating the timing missed and denied.

What part of me still savors the dream,
the shaded song I plait into psalm, turning
the melody over to a higher relinquishment,
to let dream settle into nostalgia, nodding

to think of olive-skinned women from Chios,
Nisyros, the gold-brown glistening of Caribbean shores,
to hear an old, familiar song and, half-sorry,
half-smile to still remember the words?

Plea

Psalm in a Blues Variation

What do you want me to do, Lord?
What do you want me to do?
What do you want me to do, Lord?
My only complaint is in the not knowing.
My only complaint is not in the knowing.

When called upon, I will not shirk.
When called upon, I'll respond with a hearty "Yes."
I will spring into action like a fresh lion,
like a young idealist in the dawn of a revolution.
But my only complaint is in the not knowing.

I'll do what you want, Lord.
But what do you want from me?
I have no time for sleep in a muffled bed.
I can't hear the whispering charge through
the sins in my heart and the voices in my head.

Lord, tell me what you want and make it tangible.
I don't have time for the subtle, no time
for anything to be misconstrued.
Wrap your desire for me in a clear voice
and run me through, run me through.

I know my days are brief in the winter solstice
and the distant bells are slowly tolling.
I'll do anything for your will, Lord,
but my only complaint is in the not knowing.
My only complaint is not in the knowing.

Psalm of the Modern Psalm

Lord, I want no cursing from the ancient psalms.
I don't pray for any child to have to pay
a bad price for their bad parents.

I don't wish for any sins of the fathers
to be visited upon their generations. Let the innocent
bear only the reward of their innocence.

Instead, I petition only that all offenders
be reminded of their sins every hour.
Let the selfish be haunted by their ways.

Let their eye-sockets grow dark and hollow.
The absence of the Lord's presence is a far worse
punishment than anything accomplished by smiting.

I don't focus on a God of vengeance.
I don't want revenge on my enemies—
no broken teeth, no gnashing of physical pain.

I wish the death of no one. I wish the harm of no one,
but that the Lord lead the wicked
only to repentance and a changed heart.

The gutter of their own lives is punishment alright.
But only let them realize this.
Let them inherit a living death called insight.

Psalm of No Other Recourse

Strangers I've met have chosen to be my enemies
from the very second they laid eyes on me.
Some have been inflamed to treat me as a nemesis
though I had done nothing to them, nothing.

Even priests of the Temple and seminarians hated me.
And how their greatest talent is to appear innocent.
Their faces go smooth. Their eyes widen
to work their act while I am made to appear

awkward and guilty of anything that suits them.
But I am not guilty of anything outside of myself.
I stand before the Lord and admit my sins
are against the Lord and myself.

This is my complaint: that I'm not worthy
of instant prejudice. I'm not anyone's harbor
for hatred or blame. I complain that I can't fight
back against what's invisible and denied.

What recourse do I have before the Lord
but to stand and say? What recourse
but to ask the Lord to save me from my enemies
of their own making? To let me hold my head

high in this world, through the streets and offices
opponents own. To say I've been a good person,
to know my road away from enemies, to hold
my head higher among them, and low before the Lord.

Psalm for the Soul in Depression

A Psalm of Can't and Don't, but Still of the Coming Back

This is the psalm of the useless singer.
This is the psalm of what we can't.

I can't help anyone else's sadness.
I can't even support my family through song.

Nobody can see the pain deep within the laughter
as nobody can distinguish melody from wailing.

Depression is just a mild form of anger.
So, I understand I am just angry with myself

for failing and for failing again. Then, why
do I keep struggling to get from

black into gray? Why do I focus on
such high standards? Because Jesus and the saints

set the standard for me. Then, I ask: Lord, don't
grow in anger or furrow your brow

against my obstinacy and flailing. I don't
want preaching with theatrics. I don't want

a preacher in expensive suits. There is
no salvation by slogans. There are no sound-bites

to bring us home. We don't work
with the aim for conversion. We only

witness. We don't struggle to convince. I don't
want prayers from desperation. I don't want

prayers from any bargaining. I can't breathe or function
without the Lord. I can't pray without the Lord.

I can't pray by myself. I can only pray
if the Lord leads me in prayer.

I can't make a decision for my life
without considering the Lord.

I can't do anything without recognizing
the presence of the Lord before me,

always alert, always with perspective.
I want the letting go of myself and the coming back.

I want only a prayer in the space of my heart,
saying, your will, your will, and thank you.

Then, the soul may rise from depression.
Then, the psalm may be a lifting song.

Psalm of Submission

Heavy footsteps tread through my soul.
They sound like the thoughts I obsess.
All my needs and wants out of control
till I am not blessed, I am not blessed.

Lord, take my longings from my heart
as I take down my hair to what's true.
Oh, take my list of desires from me
and leave me wanting nothing more than you.

Heavy footsteps tread through my soul
and I lie awake with the sound.
Even as a Church, we are marching
as in standstill. We don't touch the ground.

But we own nothing and take it with us,
assemble our griefs at the feet of the Lord.
I ask, when will we be good for the sake of goodness
rather than for the sake of reward?

Guilt searches for its own punishment,
as even the punishment searches for its guilt.
Even I go on with myself, when I rend
my clothes and cry for all things spilt.

Timid individuals are in a constant
fear of deprivation.
But let me give up my gripping
hold on things. I submit

to my limitations. I give up my fear of the rent.
I let go my fear of rejection.
I give you my fear of what's spent.
I give over my strife for perfection.

Heavy footsteps tread through my soul.
My voice resonates a sheminith to the Lord.
Oh, take my longings from my hands.
I wipe down my heart's bare cupboard.

We are human tears and divine compassion.
God is the gentlest hammer. He is reproof.
He is the eternity of blue water
that wears you smooth and wears you smooth.

Bless the Head of Gerald Stern

A Maskil

I call the Lord to bless his prophets,
to remember their words and visions.
I call the Lord to bless the head
of Gerald Stern, to bless even the sparce
and numbered hairs of his head,
to keep him swinging into feisty age.
Oh, bless Gerald Stern for all he gives.
The Bible may have killed all its prophets,
but not this one. You don't touch this one.
Lord, I call you to bless the head
of Gerald Stern. Let him be. Let him live
into a gloriously cranky old age with his
words to light us by, this son of Asaph,
this ornery prophet, this little saint.

Psalm as Frustration I Can Live With

I love the fierce wind outside my window
but know I would freeze in it.
I love the fierce wind from where I view it.
I love to wake and feel the Lord within.
I feel his presence only to lose it,
lose his presence only to feel it return.
I am seriousness which falls away from seriousness.
I control and lose control. I seize and lose grasp,
don't see and glimpse again.
I ration the irrational. I dive into ecstasy
and love the Lord as long as I can bear, just as
I love the fierce wind outside my window.

Psalm of Consequence

I inherit my sins in living
away from the Lord. I invent excuses.
I ruin my health from wrong choices.
I push away the people I love.

Though my voice is small,
though my heart is but one and small,
still I contribute to Shoah.
All my tiny sins contribute to Shoah.

How many are we who chip away
at the world? We are many.
What can we say to our ancestors
when we finally face them?

How will we look them in the soul
and say what we did
with our inheritance, our homes,
with the earth, this shattered jewel?

Lord, what can we say in the end of ourselves
but that we were brilliant? Though we lived
nowhere, we made the most amazing inventions.
We had the most marvelous toys.

Upon Consideration of the End of the World

"For he has made firm the world, and it shall not be moved forever."
—*Psalm 93*

And what kind of time do we live in now,
that I find it hard to believe this psalm
of the firm world to never be moved?

For man has mastered the atom
but not the wisdom of the atom.
For we can explode the world.

For we can knock the world
off its axis and incinerate everything
irrevocably. In our age now,

our seasons wilt out of time.
The cold of winter slides
into the sweat of summer,

with the briefest day of spring
to bloom anything, with no rest
for people, no rest for the earth

that groans under the weight
of its tectonic disharmony.
Even our world, even our universe

has tilted away
from the Lord's making.
Each day and each year, our weather grows

more out of control, until weather becomes
our enemy, our wild animal,
clawed in bitterness to be sundered

by man from the wholeness of creation.
Warped, we have become warped.
We have become the ruin of the pastoral world—

smudging the sky with smoke,
then with coal and the emphysema of coal,
then with radiation in the nuclear age.

Now, for every century, for every millennium,
the world goes manic to consider its end.
For every earthquake, every meteor shower,

every catastrophe and pestilence,
every resurgence of the Book of Revelation,
we remember God in our trembling

and ignore God in our mindless health.
Until our every entertainment of the world's end
becomes our entertainment in books and movies.

We consider our dying, for the rush of not dying.
Each breath in, survival. Each breath out, yes.
Until we've made an industry of our potential demise.

Yet I sing to look upon our fragile selves.
Yet I gaze with longing on this world
while still in this world.

Sometimes, the world is too gorgeous
for me to bear. I wake in suffused sunlight
and am stunned to look out my window

at the deep earth, green and breathing.
I consider all I would miss so deeply.
I would miss trees and the waving fullness of trees.

I would miss the romance of wind.
I would grieve for every woodland creature,
miss the chirping languages of birds.

I would miss ice cream. I'd miss pepper, salt,
and the fragrances of spices. God, I would miss
fresh, crusty bread from English villages.

I would miss the red and gold
turn of seasons, music, songwriting, anything creative.
I would mourn the depth of love.

And the dream of my children's children.
I would miss the world for them, the vision
of an embrace and a world to embrace them in.

There is no small loss.
Every single loss is an epic.
Every single death is a holocaust.

All we can do is sing the smallness of prayer.
Lord, consider us as we consider this world
of both of our makings. Right the world, right

our seasons, right our mindless time. Chant us
back to a psalm of assurance. Make our world
firm again, so we may not be moved forever.

Psalm in a Blues Progression

Lord, Jesus Christ is in the Old Testament
      but I specify him by name.
Lord, Jesus Christ is deep in the Old Testament.
      Still, I specify him by name.
Lord, I've read in between the murky lines
      and my soul is not the same.

I sang my witness in whispers,
      but nobody bent to hear.
I sang in sturdy whispers,
      still nobody bent to hear.
Though a slight breeze is always refreshing,
      nobody wants a wind of fear.

I know my God is not dead.
      Sorry about yours.
I know my Lord is not dead.
      I'm genuinely sorry about yours.
I just recognize any power beyond myself.
      Beyond ego, there's always something more.

Maybe think about what you got
      before you think about what you want.
I suggest you think about what you've got
      before you think about what you want.
Striving for what you can be is still better
      than complaining about what you're not.

Lord, the Old Testament's Messiah
      is Jesus Christ by name.
Lord, I've given recognition in my petitions
      to Jesus Christ by name.
Lord, I've read in between these sturdy lines
      and my soul is not the same.

ger

A Psalm of Samaras

Lord, why do I waste my time with words
when I could be silent and better with action?

Like a cold sun in winter that does not spark,
my words pale before hands that work.

I have no hands that work.
I have only a poverty of words

that don't let me do enough for the Lord.
I feel I can never do enough for the Lord,

and not ever enough for my family
or strangers, who are all the Lord's people.

Still, I want the conversation of people. I want
the flame of action, the fire that bends, tempers,

and steels—not the fire that burns and destroys.
I want the temperature that tempers the sword.

But meager, I bring meagerness to the Lord,
singing, use me for kindling, use my trunk and limbs

as wood cords. Lord, use the crumbs of me
to make something useful and better than myself—

the house we provide, the children we raise, these
scant words and shadows, seedlings in spite of me.

The Psalm Underneath It All

Lord, I gave up striving for saintliness a long time ago.
I couldn't stand myself for my constant falling.
Each breath in was guilt. Each breath out, recrimination.

I thought I was strong enough to stand for the Lord
until my strength was tested by evil, and my resolve
scattered like smoke before a breeze.

I found I couldn't stand without the Lord's support.
I couldn't even pray without the Lord's guidance.
I just wallowed in my sins, unable to move past them.

Even the memories of my past sins paralyzed me
in fear of discovery and further shame.
I lived apart from hope and apart from living.

Still, I cried, I am no longer that person.
Still, I cried, I won't be my old self.
Every night, I vowed to live the life of a good man.

Every day, I failed—but I vowed
each night again. I fought to be honorable.
Each breath in, resolve. Each breath out, determination.

I said anew, Lord, take my hands
and take my pleading.
Let me balance on my bent knees.

Stripped of every other desire
but wanting the Lord to be well-pleased,
wanting to feel nothing but contrition, wanting

repentance in all of my pleas. Underneath it all,
stripped away from every petty
thing I prayed for, I wanted

to be spiritual. I wanted to be
a good person. Each breath in
not taken for granted. Underneath it all,

stripped away, all I could ask for
was true repentance. Only that.
Let all else come.

Broken

Give me a stark and barren land
that will knock me down and humble me
             as love or need could never.
Allow me the parched sun on lost paths.
Give me the hive of the green jungle.
Lose me in the desert of the wilderness
             to drag myself through to you.
Let harsh light burn into me.
Give me the field and let me surrender
to be illuminated and broken by light.
I come to be broken.
Let me give you my shame.
To repent till repentance breaks me down.
I come to be broken.
Let me lose all but my father's name.
My back will curve into its permanent bow.
Let me starve until a crust of bread
becomes a banquet.
Let me know nothing but the miracle
             of simple, cold water.
I have only wanted to break myself
and cast myself before the wind and rain.
To die on this path, in this stark, barren land.
To lift myself again from the body of my sins.
To come wraithlike and feeble to the monastery door,
without weight of my identity.
Give me the stark way to start over,
reduced to a drifter, no worthy guest.
I come begging again to be
this broken, this blessed.

Bring Me the Head of Samaras

Lord, I bring you no words, no words
adequate. Lord, I bring you no words.

But I bring the weight of my sins, the ache
of my overused body, the tired repentance of my soul.

I'm tired of repeating myself, tired of repenting
and then doing the same insanity,

the stupid cycle of my falling and falling further.
I'm tired of the comfort and predictability of my sins.

I've been an insecure child. I've been an insecure
adult, at times. I've sought maturity, while fighting

against maturing. I've done everything but let
go to the Lord, to whom I call upon incessantly

and resist the most. I can't explain any of it.
All I bring is weariness of myself, and no words.

Lord, I bring you no words adequate.
I ferry my weariness in this world. I carry

my weariness and burden of always being cool.
I bring only this desire to stop. I produce

my feeble petition. For as long as I can,
I bring my letting go unto the Lord.

The Psalm of My Reality Now

Pay the collection notices first.

Work two jobs to cover one rent.

Then sell my books to buy food.

Weeks to go till the first of the month.

Stretch our children's clothing to still fit.

Mark in black my frayed black collars.

Remember the perception of reality is reality.

Sleep an hour or two, at a time.

Work through the humming dark.

Pay the collection notices first.

Let this one sleep away her anger.

Smile each day to make it through.

Cover my children, Lord. I learn how

to kiss them without waking them.

I Think of My Children in Heaven

Gone before we had a chance to give them names.
Gone before we could glimpse the grace of their faces—
like smoke and the lingering fragrance of smoke.
I sit in spring light and think of my children in Heaven.

How is it possible to give color to this absence?
How I pray for their lives, miscarried and missed.
My only comfort is faith their souls are full in conception.
How I feel their fledgling presence for the rest of my life.

Father of souls, I swallow hard to commemorate
each still day that is not a birthday.
Through each hour, I am a father who raises
my remaining children in this life we have left.

Nightly, the meager stars grow scant and fragile.
The stars still tremble in their glimmering light.
I hold my son's hand that is so slender and trusting.
Tucking his tiny body into gentle sleep,

I check on his breathing throughout the dim hours.
Each breath in is my relief. Each breath out is my hope.
I imagine my children's brothers and sisters equally
growing in Heaven, and pray they watch over us.

Gone and remaining, I hold their nameless names
deep within the hole in my heart.
A song for the reunion of our pulses in rhythm.
A psalm for our lives touched and lives imparted.

Book III

Movement

Against Political Correctness

Lord, we lose the country
by catering to everyone,
rather than everyone
contributing to the country.

Newspapers are written only
to sell and not report.
Television is nothing but watching
other people make money.

So, I turn off the world's trendiness.
I remain a constant man
who opens doors for women,
who is courteous but resolute.

I will not censure myself to be accepted.
I will not feel embarrassed for my faith.
I will vote my conscience, call abortion
murder, not choice——

pledge allegiance to my heart and identify
any infidels by their action and any tree
by the fruit it bears. I will pray
anywhere I want to——in school,

on the sports field, in the courthouse.
I am sick of cheap divination
and petty superstitions, the hurt
feelings of anyone else, the multipluralistic

quagmire of America.
Move on to the real.
Name God.
Open to the fact.

Naming

A Psalm for the Inarticulate

When we talk about the Lord, what God are we projecting?
When we define God, how do we limit him?

Then, there isn't "one God" when, by defining him,
we wedge him into a container of what he isn't.

Lord, we name the atom's proton and neutron.
We name the mountain "Everest."

But we can't name the Lord adequate
to contain him or define him by name.

He is only the one word without vowels.
He is the one word of only vowels.

Neither the mountain nor the atom are ample
to the Lord's majesty which takes our very breath.

What is his attribute? The spiraling
feather that eddies the air. The cloak of the cosmos.

What is his voice? The articulate wind.
The interior voice you hear whispering.

What is his name?
The trembling of water on the surface of the lake.

Naming the Lord can only be
a kind of naming. We come close.

Concealed God

What is the form of presence—
the color of wind—unseen and touching?

If we dare depict a God who is not to be depicted,
then, what do we truly have in this world?

I have no woman. I have nobody
who stands faithful by my side.

I have my children only
for the measure of their youth.

I have only the Lord's patience to keep me company.
And, hidden, God sobs to count the tears

against every depiction, every heresy, every true
terrorist who presumes to dictate God's will,

giving religion the worst historical name.
In the face of perversion, what can we do

but keep going, holding to the best of humanity?
It is the hiddenness of God that impells us to him—

even in the paradox that God is apophatic.
We wait for the times when the hidden one

chooses to reveal himself—not to be investigated, claimed
or declaimed—but called upon in faith—the one, felt thing

we do have, the breath of presence, common respect
and openness, letting everyone live.

Oh, slight form of presence—when we finally live whole,
let God be revealed to live whole within us.

Psalm as the Breath of God

Sheen of wind off the bluest harbor.
The lattices of gold-leafed light.

Anything felt deeply is a mystery, or can be.
The way theology only whispers.

The presence of God
is like breath on a windowpane. I think

of alpine wind skittered over snow. God's breath
is poetry. God's breath, the scent of snow drifting

down at midnight. Windowpanes haunted
by the gauze of curtains, the rise and fall of sleeping air.

We who practice the art of writing,
recording our feelings, in effect

put down our breathing upon the page—
breath become devotion.

The slow exhalation that is understanding.
Exhalation that is acceptance.

In this small way, we are able to capture
the breath of God—both movement and stillness.

Lord, with your breathing as my conscience,
every breath I take is one breath

closer to you. The breath that is Samaras
and is the breath of the Lord within me.

Intone a cooling breeze, sing the clarity of the desert.
Murmur the chant of the page. Oh, sing my breathing voice.

The Psalm of Fallen Babylon
and Babylon Falling

By the blue waters and long grass,
we wept for time that robs us

of even monuments, of everything
we strive to stand beyond us.

How Babylon falls.
How the hanging gardens

wither on the vine and stem.
How white winter and age

creep in to every place
so that even stone turns to dust, even names

crumble into myth
and the amnesia of myth

that fail to touch us
anymore with any immediacy.

Even I live in a nation
that winds down and declines.

How we go the way of all doomed empires
with nothing I can do but move out, escape,

call on the Lord
to deliver me from my address.

Still, I pray America doesn't go
the way of all empires. I sing

louder into the crone ears of America—
the world weeps

for where we were. By the blue waters
and long grass of Babylon, God blesses

no country more than another.
And we damn ourselves equally.

The Political Psalm

In the city of Knin, I was biblically stoned
for the crime of walking down the street with a priest.
And the hands of the throwers
were communist children's hands.
Years after we ran to stay alive,
I still carry the scar on my leg
from that day in Knin.
Now, I believe everything is political.
Choosing to live is political.
Believing in God after the Holocaust is political.
Writing a sonnet after Dachau is political.
Smiling after another atrocity
is more than perseverence.
So, I stay political by breathing,
bearing a scar from children who picked up
construction rocks in their learned prayer,
a world away in the city of Knin, near the green
valley of Saint Paul's letter to Titus.

Psalm for a Crisis of Faith

For the sight and hearing of need and help,
what can we humanly offer?

We recognize weariness.
We recognize the daily beatdown to numbness.

We admit our confusion between
worship and damnable culture.

We know we blur our sight of the Divine
by the sweat of our human struggles.

Then, how do we come
back to the faith we've deadened?

By recognizing weariness.
By resting. By stepping

back from the daily beatdown.
By letting go the fisthold on our lives

and trusting God enough.
By extending our empty hands

and letting our words be shared.
By saying language can only take us

so far. By asking for focus and focusing.
By breathing out

and breathing in.
By sharing what is often wordless.

By coming to stillness and trusting
again to be moved in stillness.

Psalm out of the Broken World

I made my pilgrimage to the Holy Mountain,
walking endlessly for the four Gospels that make
the four corners and foundation of the world.
I made my pilgrimage to the Holy Mountain

but I brought the world with me.
I dragged music in my head, each rhythmic
step of the way. I dragged my worries, the bills
still due. I carried the baggage of my living

until I saw nothing of the wonders before me,
walking through a paradise of nature,
the Holy Mountain ascending the sky,
but me multiplying the cells of my worries.

Lord, how our world is a cancer ward
and we, the mourning of a collective people,
the mourning of an entire geography.
Even the earth in tears and heaving.

Even the earth in seismic protest over ruin.
Each breath in, consumption. Each breath out, upheaval.
I made my pilgrimage to the Holy Mountain
and I tried to leave only the shadow of my footsteps.

Yet I saw the gouged paths, the color of dust,
latticing up the green mountain-face. Yet I saw
the exhaust of trucks and boats spider-webbing
the freedom of the jungle. On the broken rocks

where we docked and disembarked,
I sang the stumblings of my worries.
I sang an American psalm, a world psalm,
a psalm out of the broken world.

Lord, even on the edges of paradise, we still
wallow in worry. We live our lives in cancer wards.
We crack our knuckles and wait on the Lord.
Each breath in, fear. Each breath out, petition.

I walked the mist on the Holy Mountain,
petitioning to let go of my limited world,
calling for the white vapor of these clouds
to touch me still and touch me still.

I wanted stillness. And that was my song
of feeble longing. To break from my world,
if only for a little while. To see the world
more still, in its green stillness.

To realize the smoke in our lives is only
the smoke of our own making. Even now,
to trust that, when the smoke of the world
lifts out of the world, it will rise

into Heaven. There will be the smoke of Heaven.
There will be the smoke of prayer,
rising as incense, making fragrant and whole
what is still broken in this world. I walked on

and through that sacred space.
And each fog-lifting morning, I said out loud—
fellow souls, take your lives into the green world
that is always there waiting beyond your bills.

Go to the green peninsula for retreat and healing.
Move your petitions toward stillness.
Sing a psalm for your soul and the world.
Go to the Holy Mountain, but leave the world at the door.

Black Struggling into Gray

Lord, these years, it isn't popular
       to talk about "sin."
God is a loving God who will
       love us "just the way we are."

Other denominations have an easier God.
       But my God is Orthodox and calls me
to account for my every breath.
       So, I hold myself responsible and vigilant,

deferring the lighter path.
       Lord, I defer the lighter path.
Then, let each struggling voice
       gather to the asking:

Do you pray?
       I breathe.
Do you pray?
       I remember.

Oh, I am black struggling into gray—
       a long way to go to white.
Everything is made known by resistance
       so I resist every tempting night,

my body a sepulchre for the rising.
       I become a learner of charity,
even to myself. I become the whisper
       of the Lord in my own head, intoning

Do you pray?
     I close my eyes to light.
Do you pray?
     I pay attention.

Giving all I can to lighten myself,
     to acknowledge my sin and blame.
The way a man lives his repentance.
     The way a man remembers shame.

Psalm for Public Grieving

I grieve for the popularity of grief.
Grief in media is both singular and shared.
Then, here is the song of my public grief.

I grieve to know we are drawn to what corrupts us.
I grieve for how we come to love our deformities.

Grief to see how deeply we are in love with our sins
that we make them lifestyles.

I grieve for where our country's leaders
are the country's comic relief.

I grieve to live in a country where a verdict
of "not guilty" doesn't equal "innocent."

I grieve for a justice system that says,
If you're ever arrested for murder in the first degree,
just make sure you're a celebrity.

Grief for a society in which
only the victim gets the death penalty.

I grieve for television and music
that rob children of their innocence.

I grieve for the untold generations
of children—dead before they were born—
who are the truest souls of the saints.

They were the future inventors of cures for cancer,
for every illness we ever needed

saving from. I grieve for the salvation of inventions
we ourselves prevented.

I grieve for the suicide of smoking.
I grieve when I see the real sickness of others
and know I have no real problems
the lottery wouldn't solve.

I grieve not for the world's violence,
but for the world's finesse of violence.

I grieve for the Christians in name only.
I grieve for the Christians who receive Holy Communion
without a thought, without a shred of compunction,
who attend the Divine Liturgy as a floorshow,
the Church as a social club.

I grieve for the crowds who come for memorials,
who dress up to commemorate their dead,
but never attend church to commemorate
their own living.

I grieve for the priests who preach to apathy.
I grieve for the priest who conducts the Divine Liturgy
for the Lord, yes, and for the same five ladies who attend,
and for everyone else—absent, missing.

I grieve for those who can't love God,
can't love themselves
least of all and most of all. I grieve

for those who bear false witness
against themselves, afraid for what others might think.

I grieve for the arrogance of anyone
claiming to know God's will.
I grieve for the emotionally desensitized.

My grief is grieving, gerund and ongoing.

I am a litany of grieving,

a public list to take
these afflictions and repair them,
to take our public grief and lay it to rest.

The Psalm of Not Again

An Apophatic Psalm

Sing for the harmony between caesura and melody.
Sing of how rich negation can be,

how we may sometimes know the Lord best
by what the Lord is not.

The Lord is not an idea, but a reality.
He is not a silence, but a silence listening—

the exact space in between a clock's ticking.
The Lord is not an absence but a presence

eternal at our side, in our hearts, whom we don't access.
He is not the smoke, but the fragrance of smoke.

And I am not. I can't approach. I am parched
empty with the thirst for spirituality—

a dry sponge waiting for filling and purpose.
But I won't give up. I know God isn't a just God.

If God were a just God, we'd all be dead, by now.
Still, most people are not really Christians;

at best, they're humanists with words.
My words can't clothe the Lord.

Language can't contain the Lord's presence.
The psalm is not the singing of what we know

but the means of glimpsing the mystery
of what we don't know.

I can only harmonize
what is by what isn't.

Psalm as Tao

In order to be filled with God,
it doesn't mean I must

first be emptied of Samaras.
It just means I move myself

out of the center and give
the center to the Lord.

I'm still there, and whole,
within the wholeness of God,

a Christian Tao
united, in place,

filled with God
and not emptied,

psalm as inspire and exhale,
psalm as movement

and stillness,
psalm as psalm,

equally singer
and song.

Psalm of Musicology

Psalm of the Backbeat

I have a blues tune, a rock tune, a jingle humming.
I have a rhythm to my breathing, a guitar strumming.
The entire world becoming curled in cadence and in measure,
eight tones of the wind, tympanic bones for the skin,
hearing the treasure of the pleasure in syncopated leisure,
singing blood flow, let's go, shiver in arpeggio.
In music, all creatures call and herd, in bird call, in wolf call,
whales vibrate their words out through an ocean's wall.
We're enriched by them, romanced and entranced by them.
David danced into Jerusalem, a libation to the Lord,
a two-step, a four-step, a walk away from Imhotep, a chord
of steps, a jive alive, a musical staff and rod, a nodding
creation of air and rock, the Bible's derash and sod,
all creatures participating, exclaiming, God, God.

Psalm as Apocalypso

for Derek Walcott

Lord, give me my teacher
from Saint Lucia and Trinidad, the mentor
who sculpted the deeper

vision of my song when I was an island boy
from a different island—emerald isle, island of exile,
whose mentor still called for daylight to come,

who sang that all humans are Creole, seasoned
in language and the blood of language.
Then, all human history is Creole,

each of us slaves to something in this life.
Still, the best of us communicate through song.
We phrase our lives in music, singers

of the white rose, the testament of human spirit.
Disallowed to converse, we caroled the news
in front of masters. Free speech beginning

where our servitude ended,
choruses overcame censorship—verses
comprised of countries and cultures, souls

all singing, all singing, Lord,
our songs are the Lord Invader.
Our songs spread the news from Trinidad to the world

until we became the world.
Our songs are a string of pearls on a hot dancer.
Our songs are a rhythm of bamboo, dustbin lids

and steelpans, ricocheting our hearts.
We are a roaring lion,
the Lord Invader crooning

Canboulay, cariso, kaiso.
We rock our bodies in time.
Lord, when we sing, we sing

the world. When we sing the world,
we sing our history
remaining present tense.

Human perseverance, our songs are
go on, go on, go on—singing daylight come,
the end of fears, the end of past empires.

We are all ethnicities unto the Lord
in common applause.
Our songs are alpha and omega,

daylight and devotion in between.
Because even a joyful song is a political act,
is choice, is stance, everything proclaimed

by resistance. Alpha and omega, with
the world of our lives lived in between.
Then, croon me Greek and English, chant to me

warm island of Saint Lucia. Mentor of verse,
sing to me Stockholm, India, and Goa,
spices of song to ferry me along.

Will we have survived this life enough?
Yes, by our singing
in the face of human frailty.

Our years are one step, two step, three
step, four. Our faith is one step, two step,
three step, more. The less in this world,

the more in the next. Good teacher, we wake
and grow into humming,
may death and Heaven be a warm island

where we continue art, poems, psalms for the composing,
lives complete. Our songs incite the end of one night,
triumph of the world—daylight, daylight come.

Exodus

The Lord was as simple as walking
into evening. We stepped out of our lives.
The tea on the fire, the bread in the bowl.
My book lying face up, open at the page.
Choosing the Lord was as simple as walking
forward, the trust of a child holding onto you,
your own trust settled like believing,
the doors open onto a cool, unleavened evening.

A Song of the Going Up

Living on a mountain,
you see the vista of everything
          but the mountain.
Where is Ephratha to the south?
Where is Babylon whose gardens
we've bombed into the earth?

We stand too close to the ledge
of everything. I have seen civilization
as a plague of the white man
until I had to live on the edge of a land,
on the farthest verge from society.

High on Requa Mountain, I lived
and sat in the halo of the arena—
walking for the sight of the Pacific surf
noiseless in the hazy distance below me.

I drank from the chill of mountain streams.
I had to lie down, and pull the earth over me—
until my life became lifted shape, breath, movement—
until I tired of so much beauty.

In my days there, I could feel
my innocence returning.

Lifting myself from my earned bed
each morning now, I still claw my way to virtue.
I climb to the Keep.
I hold distance within me for everything.

I silently call upon the Lord:
let me stand before you with only good cause.
The mountain slopes incline my heart to you.
The mountain waters run like applause.

According to the Gittith

Let there be folk music to sing to the melodic Lord.
Let there be heavy wood and harmony of accord.

There was a light wind over the Mersey
and we were dancing in Constantinople.

We were dancing in Berlin and Patmos.
The world vibed from Foxton to Woburn,

doing the Cuban slide into the surf—all pacific—
below the redwood cliffs of Requa.

The twelve-string guitar works its couplet strings
on harmony and octaves

and I became a man with the moves of a dancer.
Dulcet, I danced to become water.

I wanted a heavy bass beat to feel how alive I am.
It's still amazing what you can do with

three chords and the truth to give you
your genesis, give you the whole of God and humanity.

What connects us to each other in this world
is music, melody, expression—

all of which is prayer beyond language.
Let there be folk music to resonate to the world.

Give me a song with substance.
Give me a song that empowers a body

and helps me through the heavy days
that can be that young, that light, this possible.

A Christian Psalm

When at last I journeyed to stand on the Holy Lands,
I finally understood the land of Jerusalem,
the winding alleys and warrens of Jerusalem.

Finally, I understood why
everyone wishes to possess the country.
There was something holy about even the dust.

When I lived in the compound of the Patriarchate,
I was glared at in the ancient streets,
muttered against near the wailing wall.

When I lived in the compound of the Patriarchate,
we went from Passover to Anastasis.
We laid the new table with gratitude.

Our home is built on the foundations of an old house.
Our faith is not divorce, but inheritance.
Just common respect for belief and holy dust.

No one is any apostate, infidel, or social pariah.
What are we but cousins or family members
in disagreement? I just recognize the Messiah.

The Psalm of Give and Let

Give me a song to breathe out
    and my body may be able to feel.
Give me a prayer to mouth
    and I may find my soul.

Let me give one prayer, even
    an instant of a prayer
that is real, sincere, and from
    the depth of my heart.

I give up the seconds
    of feeling good.
I relinquish the fleeting
    rush for a promise of everlasting.

I give up television. I give up
    everything unnecessary
that distracts me from living
    in the presence of the Lord.

I no longer love my passions. I transfer
    my love to the Lord. Let all the unseen present
become seen. Let our mortal bodies take inspiration
    by seeing the unseen in attendance.

Let our mortal bodies be so crowded
    by the unseen seen
that we go home changed forever,
    finally attendant in prayer.

Shiggaion

I reel about in the desert of the Lord.
I see white light without and within me.
Father, crying aloud, I reel to music unheard
but wafted on the breeze, dithyrambic and cool.
I reel about as through the drink of purest water.
Doused by swimming in this mirage's pool
of Heaven, the passion to see heat rippling the air,
as if there is heat, white light with traces of blue.
I love myself when I am nothing. I love myself
when I stop to imagine what I can be. Cry out.
Lay me in light, Lord, lay me in darkness
for light to enter my head and soul blessed.
Lay me in light, Lord, lay me in darkness,
reeling to love in this world and the next.

A Psalm in Search of Spiritual Fathers

A Miktam of Samaras,
Bearing the Universal in Particular

Lord, what has changed in the ensuing years?

I went to school with soulless children,
  all studying theology.
Even seminarians mocked me for my innocence,
  blind to their own purpose.
All I wanted was to serve the Lord and people
  pushed me away.
There were scholarships for the sons of priests,
  but I was still excluded.
Only my priest-father held me to his claim
  and supported me.
I was exuberant with life and called juvenile.
I was creative and called weird.
I wrote poems for my faith and was called
  fanatic by the priests.
Only my father and the Lord kept me
  and kept me sane.
Only my own father remained
  in the world for my sake.
Only my own father remained an honest priest
and an honest bishop. The anomaly of that.

I remember the friend who told me,
"All I ever learned in the seminary was how to hate."

Derided, I remained proud to stand
  with the unpopular and disregarded.
I walked away from the madness of the world
  and still live apart from it, as much as possible.

But what has changed in the ensuing years?
Who else can I turn to when even
      our own spiritual elders are silent to us?
When even our elders refuse to make
      the commitment of a decision?
Who are the presbyters with their own agendas?
Lord, all I can do is turn to you and take a stand.

Let others eat well at their banquets,
hide behind their busy schedules,
make no decision so they may
      never be wrong. Let them stay ethnic,
and keep the Holy Church a private club.

I will stand in the Church
      and cense the bishop's throne.
I will stand in the faith of my own father
who preached only the word of the Lord.

Lord, I will turn to you
in the silence of the elders. In the silence of the elders,
I will hear your voice, your commitment.
I will let the Living Word speak to my heart.
My heart shall stay open to listen well.

I will not dwell on the disappointment
of Church elders in this life. I will seek out
those church fathers who shun
the high offices, and live on the holy mountain.

Only I can persevere and say, Lord,
      who can I turn to, but you?
What has remained in the ensuing years

besides myself and my stubbornness to be true,
the search for true spiritual fathers, that rarity
of clear faith and practice that leads us
      back to you?

Elemental Psalm

I was salt, so the Lord mined me.

I came as a field of silvery trees
laden with olives hardened by frost,
a rough crop with some spots
tender to rottenness, some spots
coarse and unusable, bruised
and eaten on the edge.
So, the Lord cut from me the unusable
and, from the rest of me, he made pure oil.

I was coal, so the Lord impressed me.

I was parched, so the Lord planted
deeper within me, until it took
years of digging to break the surface.

I was salt.
The Lord mined.

In the darkness, there is no greater
reprieve than a spark.

In the desert, there is no miracle
greater than cold water.

A Miktam for Massachusetts

Lord, let the years and the years come.
Let my friends, those smiling betrayers,
be covered by their black cloaks of holes.
Let the years come to reveal the truth.

Let them all choke on their past words
when they said some wasted their money on me
and they themselves wasted their time on me.
Let the years come to reveal the truth—

that I was righteous before the Lord,
that I answered my calling from the Lord,
that my genuine calling bore good fruit.
Let the years and the years come.

I gave loyalty and received slander.
I gave steadfast loyalty and received abuse.
They spoke even against my own father.
They beckoned me to meet them,

and left me waiting in places for hours.
If they even showed up hours late,
I was still there and they just shrugged.
Why did they pursue me, just to repel me?

They left notes on my door, calling me
Son of Ceaseless Wonders. They made
sure to call for me only when they knew
I was absent. They only called to leave

a message and the impression
of wanting to talk, but not actually to talk.
They said I had to leave the Lord's school,
and study elsewhere, as long as I left.

But I wouldn't take in their breaths.
I wouldn't let myself be made in their image.
My image remained the Lord's, and my focus
remained on His image. I cried out,

Save me from the kisses of such friends.
Lord, let me know who my true friends are.
Let the fat angels fall further away from me.
Let the hell of their personalities be enough for them.

Let me learn the proper parameters of friendship.
Let me finally go from such friends.
I stand with the Lord. I stand and say.
But Lord, don't let their children suffer

because of parental evil. No child
should pay for their fathers' sins.
Let their children move on, as I moved on.
I held to the quiet strength of my own father.

I am no one's puppy, but my father's.
I am no one's lapdog, but the Lord's.
I invoke the name of Foxton and the name
of Woburn. I invoke the name of Requa

and the place of the sparkling Pacific.
The years came and my scant handful
of friends proved true. Ocean and earth
and my own father proved true.

My life proved true. I was golden all along.
Through the years, I stood humble before the Lord.
The cloth of my calling wove strong
as the years and the years rang soundlessly.

Psalm as the Act of Writing

On the page, we can encounter God.

I write this poem because I want God to talk.
I sing this song because I want God to sing.

Writing things down is an act of commitment.
Then, I give the commitment of my hands—

asking only for what can keep me to the page.
A prayer for support. A prayer for space and time.

I write this poem because I want God to sing.
I sing this song because I want God to talk back.

Lord, late at night, I sing to the prayer of your silence.
I write to the silence of your prayer.

Lord, late at night, I turn to this quiet work,
the song that is a poem and the poem that is a prayer.

This writing to know you by.

A Psalm for Time

O God who lives out of Time,
O God who walks with his left stride in the past
and his right stride in the present,
why are we born into relentless mortality?

Why is our every consciousness pocked with sin?
What is this force to live our lives
in the ruin of Time, the trapped, non-stop
siphoning of inescapable era?

How deeply and bitterly I weep for the past.
How dry-eyed do I cry for my youth,
mourning for every soul I've lost and the loss
of their memories, the richness of their knowledge —

that great a death to all humanity.
But what can one possibly change
for the human race, in any grief?
You can't but obey Time.

The one tsunami, the one, greatest ocean,
Time moves inside you. Time moves.
Even the ebb of our blood inside our bodies
is the same timeflow, moving within.

But what is time to the Lord? The Lord
is always viewing our births and deaths.
Only God himself wades out of
and into Time, each era, each second

simultaneous to him. Then, to the Lord
in my aging, I pray for my ancestors
in the moments of their deaths.
Tonight, it is fifty years ago. Tonight,

my grandfather is born and is dying.
Tonight, I pray for those fighting
in the First World War.
Then, by prayer, may I move

toward the Lord who lives
out of Time.
Every moment we pay attention to,
we may participate in

and transcend. Every moment, we can
become transcendent with Time
that moves within us. Oh, Time moves
inside you. Time moves.

Then, transform the years we inhabit.
From our narrative prison, what other
choice may we have but to activate
and transform the dash in-between?

Lord, let us glimpse a Time
beyond ourselves, the transcending
that the Holy Spirit rejuvenates
within us to our dying—

the living out of Time,
the imperceptible moving
that draws us closer, to finally
move us from life to life in Christ.

Praxis

Every instant, every instant moves us
      toward God or away from God.

No such
      thing as stasis.

Not even the night is static—
      the stars glitter in their pulsing place.

Not even the noon sun is at rest,
      but it ascends to the second of its descent.

Lord, you are with me every instant,
      whether I notice or not.

Every instant moves me closer or farther,
      farther or closer.

Let me notice my praxis, my soul in pendulum—
      toward you, toward you still.

Let my days and heart and reach keep moving
      toward you, toward you still.

Steps of Prayer in the Holy

I walk in the Holy, head down
but peering up, fearful to make
any noise, making my way
by inching forward.

I walk in the Holy, head down,
recognizing what is special
by my behavior and attention.
I give attention.

I walk in the Holy, over the plush
hush of maroon carpets, through
the whispers of centuries in the walls,
the solidity of air bowed to earth.

I walk in the Holy, and let
the lights be diffused for a holy place.
Let the air be transformed
and we breathe the quiet fire.

I walk in the Holy, understanding
in my depth how even the air of this place
holds presence, holds devotion, the gold
light burnished by faraway chanting.

I walk in the Holy, and the most real air touches me
where I can close my eyes for these moments,
absorbing the hymns and breathing
the incensed air, sensing I'm never alone.

Why This Church, Invisible and Seen

I walked alone over the earth of my making.
I walked alone to embrace a community.
I became a community to speak of worship, to bring
worship before myself and us together.

Alone, the Trinity inside me called
me to a worshipping congregation.
Oh, how the Church in me grows full
in the process of worship, the outreach

of my arms to interlink with others.
How I find my fullest expression
and realization through the chanting
of a Divine Liturgy, the incense of veneration:

I am continually formed to be
the mystical Body of Jesus Christ
and each of our faithful members
this renewed dwelling place of the Holy Trinity.

Together, let us be the glistening face and voice
of the Lord's Church, let each of us together
be the very expression of its inner self, we
the essence and response, we the people awake,

constantly stepping into the harmony
of light and warmth. We who manifest the mystery
of unity in diversity, let us interlace our fingers
into a community's hands, defining

ourselves, giving strength to the Lord's definition,
the Christ who gives God a face, both private and public,
individual and communal, which is why
this Church, what is invisible and seen.

Psalm of the Church in Our Century

Here, take the dark hours of dawn
thinning into morning light, light
building into a strong day.

Take the hymn of what it means
to be alive and grateful. Here,
take an ancient hymn and make it relevant.

We sing for the still sleeping, the unconscious.
We sing for the spiritually apathetic.
We sing for those who take the song for granted.

In our century, our churches are cavernous
with absence. We are spotted with the halfhearted.
In our worship, we worship convenience.

In the holy moments of Sunday, we stand
and chant to nobody else there.
We sing to the presence of invisible souls.

Still, our nave hangs onto the tremolo of our voices.
Still, we open the doors for the assembly of air.
Let hope walk in. Let remembrance remember.

We are a persistent psalm, intoning both
repetition and renewal to hold
the ancient and the modern in our heads,

in our waking mornings still given,
in our modern Church where only
the dead show up late to commemorate the dead.

Shema

I.

More than the faint fires of our good intentions.
More than burnt offerings and sacrifices,
       caged doves or bullocks.
More than the loved waft of smoke rising.
More than the petition of our petty wills.

But that we seek only the Lord's will
to recognize, accept, and accomplish.
To be made capable to accomplish his will.

II.

More than attendance.
More than the body dragged in line.
More than posture, language, attitude.

But my heart in rapport with the Lord.
Lord, in your congregations, I will show up
on time for the Holy Services,
so my appearance will mean something,
so I may show my sincerity is deliberate
       and not merely convenient.
My faith is not merely when it's convenient to me.

III.

More than contemplation. More
than meditation, the passive lying back and dreaming.
More than the self, but the self in the Lord.
More than the self, but in direct address to the Lord.

IV.
More than the thieving moon, bald-silver and irradiated,
yet still loved in its lonely company of the night.
More than the sun, more
than the rays shining forth—six points of a diadem, blinding.

V.
More than the scorch and salve of the truth.
More than enduring through human history.
More than statutes and laws, but the spirit of the law.
More than listening.

I hear, O Christ of Israel.
I take it home with me.

VI.
More than my home.
More than myself, but my children, my heart in rapport.
More than my soul, but my neighbors.
More than the heart and understanding.
More than listening.
More than listening, but like it.

I hear.

Psalm of Accountability

Sing to me Biblical words—
in a melody, let me hear it:
the only sin not forgiven
is blasphemy against the Holy Spirit.

Sing to me umbilical words.
A crime against a child
is a crime against the Holy Spirit
within the child.

Then, we are wild with outrage.
We're screams in the sacristy.
Until to all children I hear an apology,
what would help is accountability.

While nobody can help it
when snakes crawl back into the garden,
we know that individuals
are not the organization.

If a church can go wrong, then
admittance is a start of reparations.
For a church to preach forgiveness,
it has to begin with repentance.

Sing Biblical, sing refocus, sing restoration.
From blackness, bring a light of therapy.
Until to all children I hear an apology,
we wait for a psalm of accountability.

Reverence

Lord, give me the single redwood tree
but give me also the entire forest of redwoods
and their dense bodies, the breadth and depth
and inhalation of the woods to walk in.
I want the entire Pacific Ocean and its craggy
shoreline to dance on. I want to inhale the world.
I want the tangible fellowship of the mountain,
to touch the ferned paths, to feel the warm splinters
of light out on the cove and ocean, the whales
stitching through. I want all of it, the images to behold,
the fellowship to talk about it, the world of sharing,
the receiving of everything in order to give it away.

A Psalm of Samaras,
for a Prayer in Smoke Rising

I know prophesies say the Lord will end the world by fire,
this second time around. And what do I have to lift the blame
or consequence? I'm not righteous like Lot. I can't wrestle
like Jacob. All I have is the smallness of my name.

How much do I love this green and wooded world
that I tremble to imagine it gone by the blast flame
of the Lord? What can I possibly offer the only Deity
for his sparing judgement? All I have is my name

and my father's blessing. I know the world is scarred,
but even scars grow tender with time. We can be on
the side of repentance, still. All I have is my name,
my father's blessing, and the path he put me on.

Intercession for others can serve to forestall wrath.
Every new child deserves to live his life whole.
All I have is my name, my father's blessing, the path
he put me on, and the persistent prayers of my soul.

I offer straight sincerity to the Lord, surely worth
something for time to rectify. I light a fragrant spiral
of incense, the gray filament to thread me to this earth.
I beg for the world to be safe and the Guf to be full.

My whispers are confession, my tears are leaven.
All I have is my name, my father's blessing,
the path he put me on, and my soul's prayers rising
like smoke to Heaven, white smoke to Heaven.

The Psalm of Practical Application

A Psalm of the Coming Back

I'm tired of my life failing and falling.
I'm tired of knocking the breath out of my soul.

If there are blues songs of the going down and up,
there can be psalms of the coming back.

When do you realize that reaction
does nothing well?

What can you possibly change by losing control?
What part of reality can you ever alter by hysterics?

Even the Lord asked Jonah,
"Do you do well to be angry?"

It doesn't matter where you spiral down to.
All that matters is how far you can struggle

back. This is what I do in a monastery: I fall
down and get back up again. I fall down

and wobble back. What is faith, then,
but focusing only on the rising?

Even the solitary monastery inside me
is the place of confrontation.

Then, let me at least learn my right hand
from my left hand. America's Great Depression

had the least percentage in history of mental illness:
no one had the time or luxury.

So, I will myself to get on with it. I'm a blues song
coming back, with bills to pay and tears to dry.

Lent

How the earth now
struggles into spring.

How the cold hangs on,
each morning cracking to begin.

And in the evenings—to eat now
with no salt, no pepper or seasoning,

to give up any kind of leaven,
drink only water, uncooled.

How we turn off the television.
How we teach our children best

by our practice.
How we grow thin with desire

for letting go. How nothing much
is as important as we thought.

How the less we speak,
the more valuable words become.

Psalm of Waking

Good morning to the robins of Heaven.

Good morning to the sun after the insomniac hours.

Good morning to the chenille blanket that held me cozy.

Good morning to the family pictures on the wall, resuming their faces.

Good morning to the bedstead of my father and his father before him.

Good morning to my children who, with their stuffed animals,

climb in to cuddle and hold me for more minutes of sleeping.

Good morning to the luxurious stretching

of my arms, legs, and waist that reclaim the shape of my body.

A very good morning to the hazy, impressionist trees in early fog

as they rustle the blue sky into solid color.

Good morning to the birds of Heaven as I want to sing

back to them, to give them the company they bless me with.

Good morning to crumbs that feed even the earth.

Good morning to my Lord whom I wish to breathe into my being.

Good morning to my heart that lifts to the sparrows of Heaven

and my fresh chance to again make this one day right,

this one day I hope to appreciate and earn

as I step onto the green and dewy world's mantled body

and the morning lies before me.

A Psalm for the Desire of Fear

In the English language, fear suffers
from a bad reputation. But fear is what I pray for.

Not the fear of the insecure and timid.
Not the fear of loss and what loss denudes.

But Christ answers the fear of death.
And the right Lord leads us to the right fears.

The discerning fear that is prudence and preparation.
The fear of matches. The fear that is caution and care.

Love isn't the strongest emotion; it's fear.
Only in apprehension do we see our truer selves.

Fear is a way of finding our place.
Then, may we elect our reservations well.

As I choose to be terrified in the Lord the healthy way.
A heightened sense of God produces a heightened

sense of evil, so I'll be alert with fear, ever-guardful
of my soul and my soul's condition. I want to be

vigilant from fear, wired with watchfulness
so I never catch myself wanting or negligent.

I desire the fear of my death daily that I may live
each day fully. Let me take nothing for granted,

not one minute unconscious. Nothing mindless.
The beginning of spiritual understanding is fear—

where discipline begins. The awe that teaches us
our position in the bargain.

The right fear is integrated with outlook.
The right fear is totally integrated with trust.

Then, let me give the Lord and Father my good fear.
Let me be active to wake in fear and sleep in peace.

Psalm of Persistence

Lord, I want to love you and I love you.
Lord, I love you and I want to love you.

I want to repent, Lord, and I repent.
I repent, Father, and I want to repent.

Lord, ignore the music in my head.
I try to ignore the music in my head.

Prayer is returning to the prayer.
Then, all this is my prayer and the loss of my prayer.

Lord, I want to love you more.
Can I love myself less?

I ignore the music in my head
until the stillness becomes music,

until I want to repent and I repent,
until I want to love and I love you,

where I struggle to pray again, Lord,
my prayer returning to prayer.

The Old Order Has Passed Away

A Psalm of Time

What in my life do I know
      more intimately than my sins?
My long days are weary
      from living with them.

What may I do to be new upon waking,
      to air out the home and attend the Lord?
I confess my stupidities. I will remember
      my selfishness no more.

Instead, let me think of something
      other than myself.
Let me take inspiration
      from my father who still holds me.

For all the grey fathers are fading,
      the children of the Great Depression,
a generation whose strength we shall
      never see again without new repression.

What in my life do I know
      more intimately than the example
of fathers, who gave us everything and deserve
      more than what we take for granted?

What I may do to be new upon waking
      is to remember our fathers before the Lord,
to be as good as they are, confess our youth,
      providing for our children in turn.

The Psalm of Again and Again

I repent, repent, and repent of the same things
I've repented from, year after perpetual year.
Sick of myself, I despise the same things that trap me—
there are no locked doors in hell.
I struggle with the endless agony of repetition
without the symmetry of repetition.
Against the fallen human nature in all of us crying,
can rededication be sincere, each tired time?
Me promising, this time I mean it, this time
I mean it more. Once more into the breach, I step
back from the precipice. For as long as I can hold
my frail resolve, let me lift my head again and walk
back to the Lord—each same time grimacing my vow:
I want to change. I do change.

Contemplating the Nature of Hell

"Those in Hell are unable to remember God."

How I froze at reading that,
the page chill on my fingers, everything

changed in the air around me, my body
newly strange. How even the concept

brought me the purity of terror.
Since that reading, I'm unable

to sleep, and under night's dark erasure
can only think:

God, let your name remain a pebble in my mouth.

New Entry Written in Smoke
into the Book of the Covenant

A Psalm for the Language to Live On

In my language, the word *despota* has a benevolent tone.
In my language, the word *patriarch* means
        everything gentle, beneficent.
The sermons of my father taught my hands the art of language.
By sin, I am mute. By this paper, I give voice.

This pen is a conduit to the Lord.
This pen, witness and testimony.
This page is an ancient recording device
        that carries us through time to you.
This pen is address, and all of our lives to connect.

When all else is *ashan, ashan*—
then, writing is smoke on paper.

Remembrance is devotion.
Speak the words to live on.

This is a language that moves beyond history—
a language set free from history,
to be itself and representative.

Ashan, ashan.
We grab smoke in our hands
to hold onto something. We weave
substance out of smoke.

I speak them alive, my ancestors
        who are air,
who are earth and nurturing,

who nurture my body still.
As I am the body of my father
and breathe still for my father.

I write to make things real.

Our language passed through governments,
through kingdoms and the mouths of men.

Our language rose through time
to the throne of God,

became golden with survival,
rooted in the reality of all things eternal.
Ashan, ashan.

There is no faith without language.

Our language is a blue night bathed in moonlight.
Our language, given to God, was the closest to Theosis.

Still, we speak. Even in music, we speak.
        Truth to power.

We are gesture and wind, a determined smile.
We are handwriting and penmanship.

We grow old to become young again,
and our language stayed—
held on in pages, on magnetic waves.

Our language stayed,
voices captured, hearts held.
Even smoke woven

back to its body. Lord, what more
our bowing, what more our writing and singing,

the language deep within our hearts,
our palms up and open,

silence on our lips
but language in our hands?

Psalm for the Crossroads

I bought a modest house that was built on the crossroads.
I live in my modest home that was built on the crossroads.
I had a bay window view between the devil and the Lord.

The horizon of America rests on the broach of the world.
On the horizon of America, you can see the whole of the world.
The devil's got a full house, but the Lord trumps every hand uncurled.

The sun rose into my windows, over the crossroads line.
The red sun rose in my windows, over the crossroads line.
I knew what I saw, but had no words adequate to describe.

I was brought to live in America, reaching back out to the world.
I've lived my life in America, reaching out to the world.
Lord, tell me how I've lived, and for what I toiled.

Oh, live your lives in houses that are built on dusty roads.
We all live our lives, housing our hopes on dusty roads.
I lived to be sincere, and maybe I'll reap what I sowed.

I close my eyes for clarity, to ponder the soul's blue gaze.
I close my eyes for clarity, to ponder my soul's blue gaze.
What truth I may see is only glimpsed, then it flits away.

I retreat further for clarity, to hear myself in the din.
I move into the desert, to hear my own voice again.
Let the Lord whisper to me, my acts were both loss and gain.

Oh, the wind is blowing on the crossroads of the world.
The blue wind goes blowing over the crossroads of the world.
The white flag of humanity is the last flag we can unfurl.

I give away, I give away all the things I never owned.
I gave my children the foundation my father gave first to me, oh.
I give the breath of my words, and ask for mercy for my soul.

Oh, the crossroads are everywhere you find yourself traveling along.
There are well-worn crossroads you walk or stand upon.
Just keep your eyes on the Lord's horizon, and breathe out this song.

The Motion in What Is Rooted

Lord, everything I do.

My father and the parts of my father in me.
My children and the lives of my children in me.

The sliver-moon, the crescent smile.
The ocean surf at night in the cove of Hidden Beach.

When my hands move.
When the hands of my father move with me.

When the slight wind catches the length of my hair.
When my thoughts sing in my stillness.

All I am and all I breathe is movement,
for all of me and all of you.

Lord, Lord, I move toward wholeness.

It Is Not the Will of God

The losses we endure
        never leave us.
The love we birthed
        never dies.

Our losses may fade their pain
        but never leave.
Our loves remain waiting for us
        to smile in patience.

In this way, our losses
        may become comfort and trust.
In this way, our love
        may become love again.

Too easy to blame God
        for the untimely deaths of anyone.
To simple to name him
        as conspirator, unconscionable regulator

when our hearts are ripped
        out by the souls
of our children departing—
        their bright faces shining and snuffed out,

leaving us parents to the smoke of memory,
        to the photograph, the chemical fading.
The weak and desperate blame him.
        The frenzied and frantic curse him.

It is the collective voice of grief—
       the despair of a mother in wailing,
the inarticulate breath
       of a father in choked silence.

Don't degrade our children
       by calling it any
"will" of God. Call it what it is:
       circumstance.

We are the ones
       who orchestrate traffic accidents.
We are the ones
       who stumble into the timing of calamity.

Wrong place. Wrong time. We are the ones
       who nurture our bodies
through generations to illness and allergy,
       breeding our lot. We inherit

our circumstances and pass them down.
       Industrial. Timeline.
And through all our choices,
       the Lord stands with us.

Not God's will, but we who let loose the leash
       and maneuver in circumstance—
the nature of our making and the fallen
       nature of our unmaking.

The Presence of the Lord Is Floating

The Lord's care is floating.
A pure floating.

How when falling, the world
turns into slow motion.

How, when I fell, all time stopped,
leaving myself and presence.

How I seemingly floated
out of the crash of the world,

and came to rest in safety.
How I realize my place in the Lord's care.

I am strong with his strength.
I am weak in his withdrawal.

Or better said, I am weak
in my withdrawal from his constant presence.

Lord, in the communion of the saints,
I pray, float my soul to a higher place.

Make lofty my landing from harm.
Take the gravity of my sins

and make them weightless.
Keep me in your presence.

See how a man becomes floating
when he is finally living his repentance.

God of the Desert

Only in the depth of the Desert
can you see the stars so clearly.

Any place can be a Desert if there is
distance and sight, a kind of confrontation.

Even the mountain and jungle,
dense with green and clearing.

Even New York City,
crowded with isolation.

Even your forehead when you close
your eyes in light and in dark.

Only when you find yourself lost
will you confront what you value.

Only in the Desert can you see
anything distilled and pure—

God of the Desert,
your choice, your clarity.

Considering the Nature of God

A Psalm as Midrash

The difference between God's energy and essence
is we can't know God's essence.

But we can approximate his energies
and define a measure of him.

If you understand being as the conscious atoms of your breath,
then you understand God.

If you understand God as the dialogue of love,
then you understand Jesus Christ.

If you understand the transfiguration of love,
then you understand the Holy Spirit.

What is love but the desire to give and to share?
Then, you understand the Holy Trinity.

God's secret is that he lives
outside Time, while we are captives within.

We are the aging hands folding in prayer
to the endless broadcloth of the night sky.

God's foreknowledge of everything
is secondary to him.

What is primary
is that God lives with us in each moment

simultaneously. God withstands our failures,
lives with us in the moment of our failure.

Even though he is outside Time,
God lives with us in each essence of moment,

partners with us in a covenant.
In a covenant, we are no slaves.

Whether shul or secret school or Bible class,
God is the experience of us

as we experience the moment in God.
This is how we live with free will.

The Holy Spirit works through
humility, authority, compassion—

the unexpected strangers who lift you
from your falling and wait with you for help,

the smallest children who gaze up and utter
profundity enough to shame you.

Any human preaching is about discerning
what God has been up to, from the beginning,

as we entered Time to find him.
We're not here to be the word of God.

We who live in time, held in time,
are here to be witnesses

of the Father, the Son, the Holy Spirit
who live outside time and within us,

each essence, each breathing and breathless
moment.

Understanding the Holy Trinity
in Concrete Terms

I.

He was a simple, old man from a dusty century
who held before our faces a red brick and squeezed it.
And from the top of the brick lifted fire. And from
the brick's bottom welled the spill of blue water.

II.

His ordinary hand, holding the cool clay reshaped
by nature: three elements in one. His hand,
illuminated from within, flesh to golden flesh, almost
translucent—how the mystic doesn't speak, but just is.

III.

How his transfigured hand returned to being
his hand. How he gently laid the brick
back down and smiled to lead us to breakfast.
How we grew aware of that soft light in us forever.

A Lighter Vessel

Psalm of the Bringing Back

Lord, let mystery be revelation.
Lord, let revelation be splinters of light
    filtering into me as radiance through trees.

Father, ravage me with light and understanding.
Make me a lighter vessel
    to float out of my limitation.

Bring light, bring light into my head.
Bring light into my mind and heart,
    illumination welling from within.

Hammer me as an artisan hammers
gold foil, tremulous with breath
    and spun with sparkling.

Move me out of my lethargy.
Move me away from my dead weight,
    unchaining my girth.

Fill my soul with buoyancy till I am
larger than my body,
    transparent in substance.

Bring me back to the wind
that stirs the soft hillsides, revealing
    the spiritual world's worth.

Fill my soul with light
till I am golden with prayer
    and lift from this earth.

Shards of a Mirror Reflecting the Image

Maker of my making, as you move in me,
I move in you, wanting the returning, wanting

to reflect anything of you in me, desiring
only to be and only to be in you.

I say, God the unpronouncable. I say,
God the unreflectable, I am splintered in your light,

I am splintered the way streams of gold light
filter through a forest of redwoods,

I am splintered and broken the way
a mirror may be broken in the fervour of sight

for we are shards of a human mirror
reflecting the divine image.

Oh, God, Lord, maker of my making,
I am through the looking glass darkly, viewing

your holy image in me as through a veil, viewing
even my own image as through a veil,

not even the semblance of Christ in me
clear enough, not even myself clear enough,

let alone the presence of the Holy Spirit
in my dingy reflection, in what my years have covered

over myself since my holy baptism—
until I am moved to beg in this silent wringing,

Lord, Father, polish me, polish me
until I may reflect the truth of your presence.

Cleanse and polish me until I may hum
with the music of your silence,

until I may be still with your presence,
able to bounce off any atom of your sourceless radiance,

until my deep breathing may be a dance of reflection
in which I move in the stillness of pervading light.

Father, in your name and reflection, I move
into the mystic. I move into my light and my shadow,

a dance of my soul, the reflection
of my Lord in the sky, the reflection

of my Lord in the clouds, the cirriform of air,
the reflection of myself on the surface of a lake,

the water in a glass and my hand reaching for the image,
the held water in a mirror, the life-giving fountain of Christ,

cascading its spirit, its holy spirit cascading
into my moving, my soul moving into the mystic,

my moving breaking through
into the stillness of the ecstatic, the Lord as *ek stasis*,

the reflection of myself mystically
with the presence of the Lord in the shimmering of air,

the light and the shadow, the coiling
and springing into light renewed and light renewed,

O Maker of my making, until there are only
wisps of light spiraling and strong cords of light holding,

until I am no longer even my own reflection
but God and Christ alone in me,

until vision clears from the smoky shards
of mirror, vision clears and mirrored splinters unify,

until I am dancing in stillness and reflection,
silence speaking from within me,

until the only possible words of wisdom are
I have seen and *I can't say*.

Book IV

Gratitude, the Father
of Praise and Humility

Celibate Love

Children of adoption are walking divinity.
Holding hands, they are born into safety.
A single parent opens his world and gives
his held heart—where loss and sacrifice relate.
Even a celibate love is reproductive.
All spirit generates.

Psalm of Ordination

In the Order of Melchizadek

Lord, these are the words of my father.
Let the grandchildren and generations know

these are the words of my priestly father
who came to the sacred Altar and honored the Lord's place:

I emerged from the World War
to enter the public and private war of the soul.

My palms became a paten for the holding of the universe.
For the briefest hour of the world, my hands held the Lord.

My hands held my responsibility for sixty years and counting,
my right hand held my son's hand to grow in faith, as well.

I gained my son to give him back to the Lord.
I gained myself when I gave myself away.

Then, let me have no personality. Let me have
only the eyes of Jesus Christ to shine through me.

Let me be burned to clarity by the tempered
vision of the Christ, and only Christ to show through.

For the long second I am able to clearly call your name,
Lord, I am praying. For the long second that is my life,

for the long second that is my ministry, I pray
forever in the order of Melchizadek.

I have seen the absolute destruction of parishes
through those priests who fostered their own cult of personality,

as I have seen the absolute destruction of parishes
through the council leaders who served their own agendas—

they who worshipped the language of the Lord
and not the meanings of the Lord,

they who worshipped culture and deafened
themselves to the beating heart of religion.

When they didn't like the message, they changed
the messenger—rotating the priest out,

only to cruise on the new priest's honeymoon
until the same message filtered in.

To the Lord's people in each successive parish, I said,
I am here to serve you. Therefore, I am your servant.

But the true people, the masters,
are obedient to the words of the priest.

They become obedient to the priesthood, not the priest.
It is not the priest who commands them; it is the priesthood.

It is Christ through the priesthood. From the hands
of ordination, the priest becomes the movement of the Holy Spirit.

Then, through the words of the priest,
the wisdoms of the priesthood live the truth,

the beginning of spiritual understanding—
fear toward God—grants perspective, caution, and love

in the cultivation of his world. Oh, human soul,
hear the wisdom to never judge Christianity by the Christians

and never judge the Holy Priesthood by the priests.
Be peace after a World War. Be a father and a son.

Become a paten to hold eternity in your hands, together and apart.
Become a priest only if you are able to live with a broken heart.

God of My Father Kallistos

This is wisdom poetry. This is a wisdom psalm.
Let the Elders sing, this is wisdom poetry, this is a wisdom psalm.

In the deepest blue evenings, the sound of the steady
ticking of my father's clock still comforts me—

its presence throughout my life to regulate my life.
Where now I listen for the steady breathing of my children in sleep,

I remember to thank the Lord for my father.
Because a good father's soul is the love of the Lord.

My father's soul is always present tense.
The presence of my father is holy communion.

Conjoined, ontological, my love for my father
is my love for the Lord, my parent who directed me

always there. A man who loves his father loves the Lord.
Let the Elders sing, a man who loves his father

loves the Lord. I belong to the Lord the way
I belong to my father, the way my father belongs to me.

I include my love for the Lord, as my love
for any object of desire—not to possess—

but only to stay in the beloved presence.
The way one soul bleeds for another, the way my single parent

sacrificed himself to take care of me and raise me well.
Above all, I remember my gratitude, for our relationship

stays sacramental between us all our years.
I now wear my father's shirts, his belt, his coat.

I wear my father's shoes. I walk his walk to prayer and action.
Oh, God of my generations. Oh, God of my father Kallistos.

Gratitude Is the Father
of Praise and Humility

Everything good comes from gratitude.
Everything we feel is based on attitude
and our own disposition. Only we make
our lives hard. I finally learned to take
my own responsibility, to cultivate gratitude
which parents praise, humility, and a brood
of other positive children. It's true we invite
calamity upon ourselves—so, each night,
I reject the invitation of tyranny. I lie down
to cultivate a grateful heart. I thank every sown
difficulty that brought me to betterment. Please
let me remember the Lord when I know my knees.
Gratitude must be—before there is love. I see
myself clearest, in the quiet of praise and humility.

Benediction

For what we are given.
For being mindful of what we are given.

For those who grieve and those who celebrate.
For those who remain grateful in the face of everything.

For the assembly of words that links us together.
For individual speech that becomes speech shared.

For the transformations a written page may effect in us.
For those who pay attention.

For the teachers who gave us the chrysalis of language.
For the comrades of the heart who left us signposts.

For the parent who gave us the one ethic of discipline.
For the wisdom to take discipline to heart and not resent it.

For the second chance that is the writing down.
For those who know that half of poetry is silence.

For the language of breath and the breath that is prayer.
For those who wake to light and know the depths of sacrament.

For this common meal and us who bow our heads and partake.
For those who remember that "So be it" is also written

Amen.

Grace

A man who bows his head
enters a room of mystery.

A man who bows his head in prayer
appears as one who is gazing intently into himself.

One who dies among us leaves the room
but the room and those left are forever altered.

Remember the dying breath that revives,
the language that resonates in exhalation.

Remember the one life that is carried by the many.
This is the mystery of grace—

that a man who prays alone is never alone,
that we who remain in solitude gather,

that we who gather remain in solitude
yet share . . .

Psalm for the Song and the Singing

I.
The beginning of all dialogue is listening.

The beginning of elevation is understanding.
The elevation of text is the fullness of praise.

II.
If song without resonance is not song,
then how do we elevate the text through singing?

III.
We want an inflected language,
speech with a bit of singing.
We have souls in our speaking.

We don't sing like typewriters.
We don't want the swallowed sounds.

We want ekphrasis. We want
the light and lyrical sounds drawing in,
a coloration and a brightness to them.

Our warm singing is not volume.
Our singing is not performance,
but invitation to join.

We deliver a text that allows
listeners to ponder in their hearts.

IV.
For great energy is required to convey something softly.
For gentility requires strength.
For our voices lean into the emphasis.
For our singing is a journey to greet the Lord.

Our prayers are a chant to the Lord, climbing
to him by our voices, climbing as the wafting
of sweet smoke and incense rises in its ascent.
Our chanting is a way to live in our prayers.

Our singing is our confessing.
Our singing gives commitment.

All song enables the full sides of the mystery.

V.
In the phenomenon of perfect harmony,
        the voices disappear.

In accord, our voices approximate the Lord.

By making our singing human,
at the same time, we make it divine.

Listen to the beginning of all dialogue.
Listen in harmony and approximation.
Give us the energy of your attention.

Hear our voice in the name of the Lord,
this invitation to ascend,
this song, this ringing of the living bell.

Psalm as Folk Music

Lord, what I loved in this world
was the world.

My father who raised me on
Segovia's guitar and Mahalia Jackson's hymnology.

I was weaned on the creative decade's
cascade of folk and folk-rock,

my winsome women with guitars
who thrilled me through adolescence.

And now, every song is a landscape
of my living. The harmonies of Salzburg, Austria.

The solfège of wind on the Lido di Jesolo.
Each country I lived through, I gathered

the joy of chords and culture to exude—
folk music, my beautiful singers of soul.

Ask a teenager what he worships
and it will be music.

Each melody was unity ringing. Each song
was pure joy of living, pure joy

with nobody turning us around.
Lord, what I loved in this world

was this world, countries united,
the exuberance of youth

and its folk music, its rocking, its rolling,
all chorusing in praise and praise

for the living
witness, the living soul.

Invocation

If what we summon is not what we desire,
but what we are—then our petitions
must be from our best selves.

If what we give thanks for consuming
consumes us, be sure we can first
admire the art of our meal.

Take in only what will nourish.
Give thanks for bread
from the hands of friends.

Bring stories to the table
and our realest selves.
Before you move, be still.

Let the crisp tablecloth
hold up depth. Invoke
our lives and the lives

we offer back.
Give us only the lovely
lies that show the truth.

Thanksgiving

We gather to sustenance,
and what do we give thanks for
but time and space—
the chance to be alive in that?

Whatever you ingest
will become you:
a fresh air from Canada,
a person you may call

comrade on your way,
a craft, a nourishment
to say everything for you.
You will rise in the morning,

thankful for purpose.
Sit at this table in light,
choose your sustenance
and let it consume you.

Psalm as Parrisia

Boldness Before God

I have the voice of a Black Russian deacon
and growl out my croaked song of petition and praise.
All I want is a center that holds, so I bow

and come to church. Can I surprise you, Lord?
Can I resist tonight's temptation that I absolutely
know you would expect me to succumb to?

To let me catch you finally pleased, as if to say,
Wow, I didn't think you had it in you.
Still black struggling into gray, I refuse

to let my life become habitual.
After Holy Confession, we are called
to let go of sin. But only complete

trust in God frees us from ourselves
and the history of ourselves.
Disillusionment breeds in what the egotist

expects. Humility expects
nothing and is never disillusioned.
All Christ asks of us is our humility.

Then, I give my stubborn boldness and ask
for the grace of God to heal the rest.
By myself, I can change

nothing. By my faith, I can participate
in everything. Each day waking, each evening,
resting in the refrain of gratitude.

Lord, take my hands and my pleading.
I am changing the light in my eyes.
I lift my human head and sing my black voice.

It Is Good to Confess to the Lord

A Psalm for Hoda'ah

The hard part is forgiving yourself, afterward.
The hard part is letting go of your sins

after you've confessed them.
It's hard to wear your new self.

Yet I am God's salvage.
After the sacrament of Holy Confession,

I reclaim the reusable parts of myself.
I am the leftover of myself that is recoverable.

I am God's salvage.
My whole life is midrash.

I am the explanation of myself
in the explanation of the Lord.

It is good to confess
because it helps to understand in the explanation,

it helps to let go and walk away new.
I am relieved to live in this moment stepping

into a renewed baptism and communion.
Now, I am God's salvage,

excited to sleep because I am
excited to see what will happen tomorrow.

Confession leads us not
to dread the day.

A Psalm Preparing to Receive the Lord

Then, this is a psalm for the joy of fear.
Fear meaning a sense of deep awe, deep care and wonder.

Then, this is what it means to prepare for the Lord:
Though I die daily, I focus on the rising daily.

The table of every meal must be set with gratitude.
I acknowledge the sacrifice and offer my constant change in return.

The purpose was communion. The purpose
was not for just what went into our mouths,

moreso for what came out of our mouths.
We opened our mouths for the right words to come out.

We don't come trusting in our own holiness.
Our purpose is never to become worthy

but only to become conscious of our unworthiness,
to raise our awareness, help us discern.

If we think we are worthy of receiving,
then we shouldn't approach or partake.

In every Eucharist, the true celebrant is Christ himself.
We are only the cocelebrants and supporters.

Holy Communion is the true final mystery
beyond which there is

nothing further. And only two people ever meet
at the Communion Cup: ourselves and the Lord.

We draw near with both hesitation and eagerness,
focusing only on confession, on fasting,

on prayers and reconciliation.
Then, where is our reconciliation with others?

We may never take casual communion.
Then, it's worth repeating:

The basis of beginning a spiritual life
is the discipline and insight of fear.

To die to sin and rise a measure higher.
Then, this is a psalm for the joy of fear,

trembling to receive the fire—
with the fear of God, faith, and love, draw near.

According to the Daffodils

The startled blanket of yellow on green.
The startled spring that woke our hearts.
The silent blossoming that came overnight,
giving the world back to us out of slumber.
The green stems swaying in unseen wind.
The slight bending that does not break.
The pure splash of yellow that is golden.
The pure splash, the breathless vision.
The presence of our hearts made visible.
The vivid fields and hills spread with yellow.
The colorful world given back to us.
The signature of God when we aren't looking.
The simplest miracle of daffodils to greet us.
Our gratitude in the offering of quietest things.

The Psalm of Wind, of Zephyr, Sirocco, and Kaver

And the way wind inspires me.
And how I love

the strength of wind in the height
of spring and autumn.

How my child's heart still tugs
to behold the sight of colored kites

soaring in the resistance of wind.
How gales can be thrill and inspiration

this side of safety. The stoutness
and stiffness of a warm wind

can be a friend reminding us
of the pleasure in God.

All we desire is the measure of wind,
robust but not too fierce.

We wish the joy of wind
and not the destruction, not

the too-Biblical. We give
thanks for just the play of wind,

the exotic names of wind—
Zephyr, Sirocco, Kaver, Mistral, Katabatic—

how many personality types of wind
there can be. And we become

the love of hills, of crests, whole skies of wind.
We name our loves by them. We name our inspirations.

Winter Psalm

Sing of the way to walk in prayer
and the element of prayer—
to be physically aware of where we are
and inhabit that space—to stop our lives

long enough to reconnect with the earth,
to live where we are (because most people don't).
Remember the momentary joy each season brings.
Remember the first time we ever saw snow.

Live north enough to be briefly cold.
Let our breaths be visible, riding
out of the shape of our bodies.
Let us see our breath as our visible souls.

The chill air can feel good on our bodies.
Walking and lifting our heads to the night sky,
we can say thank you for the clarity of stars
as that clarity becomes more rare in this world.

Thank you for the the thread and filaments
of constellations, their celestial net of pearls.
Thank you for the freshness of air as if breathing anew.
Thank you for the fragrant tinge of woodsmoke wafting.

Thank you for the chill only enough to enjoy it,
to feel more consciously alive as we walk
through the rare night into our warm homes.
Oh, to live in a place untouched by light pollution.

Everything in measure is everything in appreciation.
Let the Lord in by walking out. Let creation
reconnect us. In open air, there's a chance for encounter.
In the North, there is snow.

To the Choirmaster

I convene the spirit of the song and the singer both.
Lord, we convene our best when we practice harmony.
Two-part harmony is the Lord and ourselves.
Three-part harmony is the Holy Trinity.
Four-part harmony is each Gospel together.

If there can be the billions of voices harmonious,
then the world may unwobble from its discord,
the celestial choirmaster can raise his baton
to synchronize the stars, the warm wind
through the bars of trees. Harmonized, sing us whole.

Light Visible to Faith

What is our encounter with the living Lord?
Who may actually see the Lord?

There were the pure in heart
and the broken in spirit.

As I have lived broken.
As I have given the poverty of my prayer—

walking on, expecting no answer,
no Damascus Road.

Many are those who seek the Lord
but don't see him.

Many who discount
the attitude of their hearts.

It was only to those
earnest in heart.

It was only light visible to faith,
the opening first to receive in turn.

The One Hundred and Nineteenth Psalm
of America

I gave up my country. I gave up my thatched home,
dragged by boat over the flat Atlantic, over
the drowned bones of slaves and the unwilling, arriving
disheveled in America like a promise from the Lord.

So many states united, so different in region.
So many huge cities and people in legion.
Were all the songs of America the same song?
Were all the lyrics of America a lyric to the Lord?

What is the song of America but vista, the gold
grained expanse of prairies, the height of granite,
and the frothy, spirited mane of the Pacific?
What is the vista of America but where the Lord lives?

Oh, legion upon legion, what is our song but tribal?
The chant of the first Cheyenne, the human beings.
The dirge of the immigrant became our heartbeat.
The song of the slave became our blood and blues.

As we built the far stitching of railroads, we built cities.
As we built cities, we built churches that aspired to Heaven,
that stained the Heavens with their prisms of light,
that sat the universe on the Orthodox cupola of the earth.

America is the one country of vista.
America, the Pisgah sight. Even our architecture
is based on windows and the expanse of vision.
Understand the gazed-upon vista, the American land.

Yet the sleep of America woke us in generations.
I, too, grew up in the dream of America

and lived in a restless sleep—in which America
became both the gold of time and its tarnish.

Oh Lord, I lived in America
when the enemy was Russia.
I lived in America when the enemy's
name was Communism.

I lived in America when, as children,
we were taught to stoop against nuclear attack,
under our desks, covering our necks, and praying.
I lived in America when the enemy was others.

I daydreamt through the sleepy decades
when the souls of children were harbored,
when their souls were held innocent for a time.
Yet the sleep of America woke us in generations.

Each generation, marked by foreign war.
Each decade, turned to domestic strife.
Yet the sleep of America was finally woken
by parked missiles and banging shoes on lecterns.

But, Lord, our country became
a five-year-old with nuclear weapons.
We fell in love with the sleekness
of our hairy forearms.

Don't tell me this world is too modern. Our century
is merely the Roman Empire in better clothing.
Every breath in is comparison.
Every breath out is propaganda.

Every year, we are on the verge
of century, of time, of change.
Still, we are drawn to what corrupts us.
Still, we ignore what remains the same.

The worst thing a nation can possess
          is righteousness.
And now, the war goes badly.
As all wars go badly.

Everything about War is aftermath.
Now, I live in the postmodern and fragmented
states of America when the enemy is ourselves,
and the name of the enemy is our own.

Lord, I've read the world's history books.
The past just isn't what it used to be.
Now, the greatest enemy of America is time.
The greatest enemy of America is America,

for we slowly erode ourselves from within.
Every adversary of America knows all
they have to do to defeat America
is to outwait us.

This, from our own history.
This, from our running-dog past.
The distance we've come, the records we've left
behind. And only the best enemies study us, first.

Each breath in is ammunition. Each breath out
is criticism. Even the voices in Lafayette Park

protest against the injustice, the duplicity—
decrying the hypocrisy of our democracy.

And the rest of us live like muted pigeons.
We spend our lives working jobs we hate
and go home just in time to sleep, waking
to perform the same numbness again.

Father in Heaven, our culture accelerated
so much to achieve the moon, we raced
both ahead and beyond ourselves.
After we conquered the list of enemies,

the only antagonist left for us was ourselves.
Our society became disposable.
Our food became fast
and we forgot the meaning of fasting.

Our comedy grew shorter
until the punchlines were soundbites.
Now, patience takes too long.
Instant gratification takes too long.

Forget about prayer and the interaction of prayer.
Forget about the patience of prayer.
Forget about giving the Lord time to answer.
Forget about the very sackcloth of time.

Our children don't learn patience, anymore.
Our society breeds our children to express frustration.
We grew to mass-produce "self-esteem"
in the worst way: when it wasn't earned.

Everything of America grew to its own
warp of mass proportions. Lord, our culture
today even has the capability to manufacture
flowers, the small creations of our earth.

But our roses and carnations are so
mass-produced now, they have
no fragrance left, barely a hint of fragrance
bred out: all volume, no substance.

They are the petals of flowers, without
the spirit of flowers. We warp the world
we create in our own image.
We all circle sin in America, mass-producing

even the cities we live in, hiking every rent
until there's no place left in town
for a poor person to be. Is there anything
new in our age besides the toys?

Perhaps only the intensity, and even
that mass-produced. As well as we're capable
of mass extinction, we're now capable of killing
the entire planet and ourselves worldwide with it.

When people grow thin from hunger,
        we call it fashionable.
When infants are murdered in vitro,
        we call it choice.

When parishioners pass a tray for crumbs
and neighboring churches cut each other's throats,
      we call it reality.
But Lord, save me from this time I live in.

I call upon the Lord to save us from the time we live in.
Even spirituality is not fashionable, these years.
We live in an American age
popularized by trendy atheists.

They lobby and legislate the Lord
out of our schools, off our coins,
and out of our governance.
How many generations have been like us?

Our diet, deadly as refined sugar,
our food, damaging as processed, white flour.
We are a culture of dissatisfaction— .
overwhelmed, stressed.

People's agony has become their passion.
Even I was affected by the American dream,
when I was embarrassed by where I lived,
ashamed to bring any friend home to visit.

Still, the political strives to break down
any structure that could be
stronger than itself.
Like Family. Like Church.

Politics is a separatist entity.
Until there are two great temptations in this world:
        nostalgia for the past and despair for everything.
Neither adequate for our souls.

Let our nation return to the laws of the Lord.
Let America return to the innocent decades.
In our generation, we have long memories.
In our generation, we have an intense

thirst for a lost spirituality.
There are still things beyond the creature's politic.
There was always a center, always
grounding for a nation underneath us.

And when we personally fell apart,
there was still a center elsewhere.
All we had to do
was live in that choice.

I ask the Lord to bless our people
again, as once before. Even when I was
a missionary in the darkest continent of America,
a flower-child, folk-singing infiltrator to change

the system—frustrated because I could change
nothing. Still, we are soul-searching people.
We have an intense thirst for spiritual endeavours.
Because we live in a constant, low-tremor earthquake,

we desperately need the discipline of Hesychasm,
the one stillness in which we may move.
All you nations, learn from this.
Learn from your own histories,

your litanies of failings, your risings and crumblings.
Roman, Byzantine, Ottoman, British, Amerikan.
Go to a small country. Ask a man in a field
what country he is most afraid of.

God, we have crippled ourselves following
inevitable history, hobbled ourselves
by ignoring history. We bring to the world what we possess—
and it is usually insecurity and anger.

But who was it who said, Prophets don't read the future,
but the present? History is always only
what is about to happen.
Then, let us be historians of the future.

Let us bring back to the world our best selves.
Let America remember hope in the Lord,
as it did when America was born.
Only humility can save us.

Love made the world both large
and small, at the same time.
I still want the fragrant echo of smoke,
the incense spiral, the gray filament

to thread me to this earth. I want
the music of hymnology to hold me whole.
Let us return to roots music. Our music genres
are our identity, spirit, our national dignity.

The American psalm can become
the world psalm again. For America holds
the world in itself—holds a home for the world.
We just have to remember

the patches we were woven from,
the many countries welcomed here,
the broadcloth quilt that came from the weaving.
America remains the greatest horizon

before the Lord's world and creation.
America remains the space of the world.
Lord, from our country, make us
a sacred space, a sacred space again.

Let's keep the Sabbath again, a day
of rest, reflection, and family.
Bring back the front porches of our architecture.
Bring back dialogue with our neighbors.

Return our recognition of divine laws
that allow a place for the Holy Spirit to work through
compassion, humility, and authority:
        three things America has lost.

And we say, Lord, return our country
to your sovereign care.
We are the voices of multitudes
searching for human harmony.

Even in our broken way, we make music.
Even I, with one splintered voice, say,
Son of man, I am a son of man
among all of us. Lord, I pray to you

in my crippled way.
Citizen of nowhere that lasts,
I pray to the permanence of wind.
Citizen of nowhere, I make a country

of gratitude. Let me come to rest in gratitude.
We all began in breathing. We all held
breath between us, leading to cries of petition,
however unfocused. Lord, let us journey

from the foundation of breath.
Let us use petitions as mortar
to refine a true movement. Let us build
walls of gratitude to settle into homes

filled with an air of the holy.
Lord, rebuild the towers—turn them
into towers of our faith in you.
Let the psalm of America be sung.

Let the American psalm become the world psalm.
For America is a stubborn hyphenate—
remaining the greatest horizon
before the Lord's world and creation.

Look at the multi-colored threads
of this world, its living braid.
Even I become the bond of the world—
made stronger by its weaving.

I am the good dream of the League of Nations.
I wave the United Nations flag because I love the idea.
I sing the anthem of this world. How I grew
firm by the thatch of England,

always a red poppy vested in my lapel.
Here, I stand on the foundation of Greece that once was,
a history in beautiful ruins. I am the education
of Chambesy, Switzerland—the harmony of languages

drifting over regional borders. I am the peace of Sweden,
my dream of Sweden. I am the humility of Mother Africa.
I am my American brother with a raised fist.
I am everything that has influenced me.

My vision is the clarity
of every desert in this world.
I am the wild surf of the gorgeous Pacific.
I am the peace of all the pacific fathers.

I attempt the world because I love
every leaf of this world. I attempt the world
because we can actually choose imaginary borders
connecting country to country, soul to soul,

the divination of landscape braiding into landscape,
the earth we inherit. Ply our nation with prayer
to become a plait of prayer answered
in the presence of the Lord.

Keep the presence of the song. Hear it: a chant
across oceans. Hear it again: a blues refrain
that enlivens, that brings back, brings
back endurance for living on and giving.

Sing it, gratitude. Sing it antiphonally,
gratitude again. For I am one soul
within this world of countries reaching
out and without, an American psalm

to a world psalm, a poem for change
and return to innocence, a psalm
for perseverance. Then, hear it
finally—a prayer for forgiveness

and humility. Hear it again—
a singing to lose and find ourselves,
a singing for faith and country,
a song for the kingdom and kingdom come.

The Song Holds the Moment Forever

Thank you for words and for the pause
of words. For refrain and for refraining.

Thank you for the commitment of the spoken,
for the silence that gives weight. I am grateful

for the chance to live, and what I did with it.
Thank you for those who love me, the father who raised me.

Thank you for the days and the beauty of night.
To stand under the dusky body of the universe.

Thank you for the vision to look up and dream.
Above all, thank you for the stars.

Sustenance

The Lord said, "Here is a wooden table
you assemble yourself. Here is a plate
of words, seats for company and conversation.
Craft them well. Others may starve
for what you are given from banquet
to banquet, the pen, the fork and knife,
the daily bread. The years will fill you
if you carry the refrains, at your made table
where even the memory of a meal sustains."

Psalm for the Consolation of Israel

To the lifting of Symeon's hands
in raising the infant Christ.

To the lifting of Symeon's hands
that bridges everything intertestamental:

the Old Testament in his left palm
and the New Testament in his right.

To the vision of the apostle Peter.
To the vision of Peter again, covering the world.

To Rachel consoled and united with her children in Heaven.
Now transformed as all of us.

Now traveled through all of the modern world.
Now holding the ancient in the carry over.

To Symeon who grew elderly in his faith.
To the lifting of Symeon's hands.

To all of us, inheritors
of gesture and faith.

To Israel in Arabic homes, in Christian homes,
in the transfigured world.

To Israel in forest and desert, metropolis and village,
in the heart of the Messiah here, present

and accounted for. Now our hearts
in the heart of the Messiah. Now our hearts

in the lifting of Symeon's hands.
Now gratitude for recognizing

the promise fulfilled.
Now every believing home is Israel.

Psalm in the Words of a Simple Man to Emulate

I do my Cross in the morning.
I do my Cross in the evening.
In the middle, I say "thank you" a lot.
In the middle, I say "help me" a lot.
I remember the island I came from,
so I do my Cross in the morning
and go to work where everything
I touch in the day is a blessing.
I know there is this presence taking
care of us, as I work the light and dark
to earn enough to provide for my family
and then wind home, wind home to them
where I do my Cross in the evening
and I do my Cross in the morning.

Lord, Is My Life Long?

A Psalm of Time

Lord, is my life long yet?
I still feel like a lad, a child myself
for whom the world remains
fascination and awe.

I never lost my wonder for this world.
I never lost my marveling at trees,
the thrill at hearing morning birds,
the faith of having my father at home.

Lord, my Father, is my life long yet?
I raise my children and feel
like a child in their love and laughter.
I see how they love me without condition.

I see how they love me purely, as only
my own father ever loved me purely,
expecting nothing of me, wanting
nothing of me but my love and attention.

I am attentive and love them all.
I think of my other children in Heaven
and pray. I pray daily and then increase it.
I commemorate them with all my time left.

Lord, keep me safe in traffic and travel,
keep me safe from illness and pestilence,
for the sake of raising my children
and the sake of my repentance.

Lord, is my life long yet?
I feel each breath in me, ticking.

Time moves inside us.
Time moves.

What makes an antique
        but time and passion?
What makes a hymn
        but time and passion?

What makes this prayer sing
        but heart and soul?
The Lord answers humility first.
Then, let me grow humble in the years.

Let me live long enough to become nostalgic.
I become the aging hipster
with the vintage clothing, the dusty
sandals and beads, the closet of memories.

I mark how the generations comfort us.
How we remain the remnant of ourselves.
Even ninety-year-old fathers may still
yearn for their fathers.

Lord, is my life long yet?
What age have I ascended to, thus far?
The skin on my hands has gone
gold with the texture of parchment.

Time moves inside us and
we can't but obey time.
Don't think we can outlast all the days.
Don't think we have real time to pray.

Lord, like eternal music from our adolescence,
I save my lifetime of regrets,
praying my regrets can only be outweighed
by my lifetime of gratitude.

Lord, is my life long yet?
We are in eternal search for meaning.
The many of us who are not afraid of death,
but are only afraid of dying.

What can we do with a death, but celebrate?
What can we do with a death, but thank
the longish time? May I outlive the history
of my resentments. May I outlive my hatreds.

Lord, my life is yet long.
And I've held the secure feeling
from my father's hands, faith and security
from the gold parchment of his hands.

Lord, I've given my firm hands
to my children both, given
myself to the longish eternity,
given all of myself in final love,

my life yet long, facing reunion
with all of us in age and era bending,
where we stand of our time,
of the living and the ascending.

Psalm for the Afterlife

Father in Heaven, which man has the greater hope?
The man who is dead or the man who is yet alive?
Let everyone ask in this world, which man has
the greater hope—the man who is dead

or the man who is yet alive?
In my youth, I answered, "The man who is
yet alive—for even five more minutes of life
is five minutes more in which to repent.

A man alive has the greater hope."
Yet the answer came—the man who is dead
hopes more—for he is the one who now sees
the reality of God before the throne of God.

How I was stunned by that answer.
How everything I knew was all theory
in the face of a dead man's reality.
Oh, I am dwarfed by the Lord's magnitude.

I can't comprehend his largeness,
his accomplishment of creation,
his caring still for the smallness
of my soul thrown into the maelstrom.

I admit my faults.
I know I have sinned to infinity.
I've constantly kicked myself for my sins.
I know I've kicked myself far

better than any of my enemies could.
I know the reward of all the times of my stumbling.
When I was born, I was born
into the ticking of my death.

Soul, I say soul.
Soon, all that will be left of me is my soul.
Soon, I will say goodbye to my body
that has been both my enemy and friend.

I give my hair and my beard to the ground.
I give my hands to the ground. I lie
down and give all of myself to the Lord.
I give my constant weariness to the earth.

On my dying, my only sorrow
will be for my children.
On my dying, my only sorrow
will be for my daughter and son.

My only sorrow will be for my not being able
to see trees and birds anymore.
And for not being able to write poems anymore.
Maybe they'll let me write poems in Heaven.

Lord, as I die, let my children hold my hands.
For it was my daughter and son who made me mortal.
I never got to meet my grandfather,
but I will meet him after I die.

Oh, Lord, let there be windows in Heaven.
Let my soul stand by my children's sides

for the rest of their lives,
even if it be only a minute of eternity for me.

Let me protect them, let me sigh in their growth,
to pray for them always
as I pray for them always,
as I give thanks and gratitude for everything.

God and Christ brought us salvation—
but no one is saved until the day of Judgement.
Let me blink, then, through the passage of Time
which was my life I gave to repent.

Heavenly Father, draw me near.
After my death, Lord, let there be no grieving.
After my death, Lord, whatever your love wills for me.
Lord, Lord, I am only as far from you as this breathing.

Book V

Stillness

Silence Is Not Stillness

What have we inherited from this modern world but noise?
Our legacy: machinery, a constant hum of electricity, distraction.
All the world's loudness.

Yet diminished, there are still places for retreat.
God is active in silence,
the plane on which he interacts with us.

When we come to silence, we are busy listening.
When the Lord is silent to us, it is most probably
that he is waiting for us to say the right thing.

Then, I bring patience
to myself in the noisy world.
I cultivate silence. I harvest

the lengthening of moments distilled, decanted.
To confront the noisiest place inside,
I am actively quiet, in the work of quiet.

I seek that voice, that whisper,
presence.
Listen.

I am practicing silence now.

Stillness Is Not Silence

Hesychast, surrender.
The inward thought. The inward silence.

Be still inwardly, as a regular practice.

In the form of stillness, see and hear
everything.

The Alone of My Time

A Psalm for the Blessing of Solitude

What will I do in the alone of my time
but bask in the solitude, the crowds of domestics

quieted, removed? What will I do alone
but praise the solitude? Oh, solitude, my love

for solitude. You best
meet the Lord in solitude.

May I sing in the alone of my hour,
as I take Time and make a friend of it,

as I move within Time to maximize
my moving toward the Lord.

May I sing for my father who raised me
well to be secure in solitude, to wish

for nothing but security in our Lord.
Lord, may I sing contentment in the quiet moments,

gratitude for the world slowing.
May I sing a stilling hymn

in the retreat of the soul alone,
in the body at rest, only in contentment,

in a too-modern world where being
alone is an accomplishment.

The Acceptable Year of the Lord

Κηρῦξαι ἐνιαυτόν Κυρίου δεκτόν.
"To proclaim the acceptable year of the Lord."

Why do atheists get off work for Christmas?
You'd think that, if they were at all committed,
they'd absolutely insist on working on Christmas.
They'd sue for the right to work on Christmas Day.

All I see is that atheism is merely another theism,
in which man worships himself. Since atheists mark
time by themselves, why don't they then lobby
to change the years we live in, the calendars we use?

What year this is depends on who you ask.
The year of the dog. The age of Aquarius. The year
of still waiting for the Messiah. All I know
is I mark time by God. I follow

the Christian Calendar because I believe
in commemoration. I believe in Sabbath weekends,
in holy days serving to give
my life meaning and order. With Jesus Christ,

I can understand the past and the future.
I can understand our human place.
Only faith stands up to Time.
Only faith can even define it.

Knowing Intimately What Can't Be
Expressed

For those who exist but do not live,
no words suffice.

For those who feel their every breath
and flow of blood, no words are needed.

I gaze at my open palms, and their lines
reach back through the centuries.

I see my father, my grandfather—
back to the unknown names who made me.

I feel the intimate atom. I approximate
an Absolute, and am betrothed

to my conception. I am united, joined by essence
to what I can't express but can only feel:

this innateness, this presence in my body,
this clear vision to which words

give no justice and have
the color and substance of wind.

Octave

A Song of the Going Up

In sleep, your breathing was open.
In white sleep, your voice, resonant with depth and rising.

In sleep, the white moon rose whole through the window.
In slumber, the skirling clouds listened.

Listen.
Our attentive listening to God is a form of prayer.

Deeply integrated human beings,
we must give voice to all we have within us.

This climbing. This scaling.
The soaring depth and ascent.

Listen to the nothing,
the stillness in which you grow aware.

I open the window on sleep
that is the letting go of everything holding us down.

I open myself to hear
the voice and the voicelessness of the Lord.

Everything in Existence Is Dialogue

Blue sheen of lake and blue air
that is the skin of lake and not lake.

Hand weighing a gray stone.

The seen wind that trembles.

I tell you this—

The Greatest Line of Poetry Ever Written
in the English Language

"He said, and stood."
—*John Milton*

The Lord at Haran and the ladder of Haran.
The Lord on the crags and in the crevices of Sinai.
The Lord on the Mount of Temptation.
Jesus Christ on the anonymous mountain.

The Lord on Tabor.
The Lord in the oasis of En Gedi.
The Lord in a pillar of clouds, standing
in the door of the Tabernacle.

The Lord between the living and the dead.
The Lord on the plains of Saskatchewan
and in Thompson, Manitoba.
The Lord, the Lord said and stood.

And I stood at Horeb.
I stood on Patmos and faced the Apocalypse.
My spirit stood with Darmok and Jalad at Tanagra.
I stood with Shaka when the walls fell.

But I stood in Quincy and claimed my father.
I stood in Brookline and wouldn't back down.
Determined, I stood unswayed before the small rulers.
I stood until there were nails in my heels from standing.

Even when I knelt, I remained
standing before the Lord and no
seminarian or priest or bishop could buckle me.
I left them fumbling at the river Temarc in winter.

I stood as my own father stood—
upright, unflinching.
I stood in humble resolution
before the Lord on my knees,

nobody but the Lord knowing my spirit resolute
and how I rise and rise again, remembering
the Lord in the Temple of his own,
the Lord at my side

while I pray to stand in right glory,
stubborn in a good way, to claim
the event and the place of the event,
to say and to stand, and be at rest.

Psalm for the Long Memory of God

"These are the days of miracle and wonder.
Don't cry, baby. Don't cry."
—Paul Simon

Lord, remember Samaras, the tiniest soul.
Recall the small flame of his sincerity.

Remember the quiet strength of his stubbornness.
Re-member his patchwork of prayers, stitched

by human breath to divine breathing.
Remember his petitions for the largeness

of the world made small. Remember Samaras,
as all souls are unique.

Remember he who served and fell
and rose to serve more.

Lord, Father, remember Samaras and his father, Kallistos.
Remember Samaras whose birth was worth

something to the Lord, if not to the world.
Remember how we lived

in the presence of the Lord, even if we could
barely perceive it. Remember Samaras

who moaned his breaths of longing
for the Creator,

who longed for justice, for righteousness,
for human kindness, some kind of compassion,

who grew venerable with longing and restraint.
Remember our modern times in which we lived

and lived through, persisting, bringing
into the ages our pure potential, giving

our children the chances we squandered.
Lord, remember what we gave birth to

and what we survived, these days
of miracle and wonder, these days of weeping,

our wonderful, lethal century,
our brilliance and blindness.

Remember our shortest memories, our long
history that is a blink to the Lord.

Remember that our origin was in the Word,
that our words wended back to our origin,

our breath, our spirits, our stillness unto knowing.
Lord, remember the civilizations we built and destroyed

and built again. Remember the ecology
we finally came to, the clean streams

we cultivated and returned to, our one step
forward and our two steps back.

Remember the waters of Babylon we buried and dredged.
Remember our holding on for desperation,

our holding on for love.
Lord, remember us in your long memory.

Remember Samaras, son of Kallistos, who breathed
his way to gratitude, who moved his way to stillness,

who worshipped in an active contemplation,
who pointed the way in poetry, in a lyrical

breath of song to ring through the years,
who rose like the smoke of incense, who gave

everything he received from his own father,
whose fruits of his tree were words and the work of hands,

the lived words, the verse's silent song,
the humming stillness of the written.

The times, the living, and the resting.
Lord, remember.

Abide

Because you abide in me,
I abide in you.

In all definitions, I live with you
in an intransitive sense. I sense you constantly.

Uppercase or lowercase, you are still intimate.
With your presence, I am still.

I endure without yielding, bear
everything patiently, and accept

without objection
your one, enduring reality—

your presence.
And in your presence,

I am language of blood flow.
I am inhalation and oxygen,

resonant verb of your company.
Nothing else

this constant,
this abiding.

Heart and My Heart

Two for the sharing, the pulse in unison.
Two for the dialogue implied in it all.

Two for the lips that press to pronounce words.
One for response and one for the call.

One for agreement on what words signify.
Two for the language that answers accord.

One for the writing and one for the reading.
Two for the grasping, the holding in turn.

One for the murmur that trembles the blue air.
Two for the hands that mirror in prayer.

One for the lamplight, one for shared silence.
Your heart and my heart, the sacred text of this.

Psalm in Translation

How can a mortal express anything adequately to the Lord?
What words represent exactly, in a language of inexactitude?

Everything is made known by comparison.
But the stars of Heaven don't reflect on themselves; they just are.

Each day for us is transubstantiation.
Each day is the process of turning, and we are the turning.

I am the culmination and sum of my days.
The Lord is the scribe and accountant.

Yet what do I have sufficient to that balancing?
In what passable language may I find justification?

Forest air and woodsmoke, translate my soul.
My father's broad arms and smile, translate my soul.

Bird language and bird dialect, totems of what I love.
Pacific Ocean and the cataracts offshore, represent me whole.

My father's silver hair and white beard, translate my soul.
I can give the world only those things I love, to know me by.

I raised secure children.
I tucked them in and kissed them every night, *goodnight*.

My daughter and toddler son who hug me, render my soul.
Hymns and sermons of my father, explain me whole.

Folk music and lyrics, my breath and blood. Bookshelves
lined with the volumes of my life, my depth and wood.

A meadow of waving daffodils in England, interpret
the spirit I extol. Deep fields of Foxton village, thatch

my heart and essence, my goal. Sedge of fern and redwood forest,
decipher my character. British politeness and Greek rhythm,

proclaim my steady toll. Calm of night stars and calm
of pacific waters, reveal me whole

to all I was and all I am, a man
before the Lord, a living soul.

The Monastic Psalm

A Psalm in Antiphony

Every time you pray, a demon screams.
Then, let me pray my way through noise to stillness.

Every wounded ego cries out for Hell to soothe it.
Then, let me have nothing of comfort and amnesia.

But give me a trinity of years to end my life
in the place of the orchard and glare my way to truth.

Evil is always invited.
So, let me close the lights and be at home

with no one but the Lord.
Everything is made known by resistance.

So, let me occupy the night with nothing
but the attentive tilling of my soul.

Let me continue to resist in the small, significant ways.
To change the world, I change myself.

World Psalm

How the breathing refrains of music—arioso—
spread like continental air in the slipstream,
oxygenating the planet, a vibrant sheen
greening the four corners of a round world.

How the American psalm becomes
the world psalm—an anthem holding
the world in itself, containing
a home for the world. America,

the melted and musical, joyously mulattoed
in jazz and blues, remains the one open horizon
before the Lord's creation, the one country medleyed
on the cultures of all countries, all immigrants.

Give us three hundred years of a nation
and we turn back to the world we sing witness to—
even pitched and off-key, we struggle to return
to the staff and signature of harmony.

Even for America now, we live
in an age of assassinations.
Even in the brief span of my young lifetime,
we've graduated from assassinating our politicians

to assassinating our poets and singers.
And the larger world goes on killing itself—
children dead in the crossfire, parents
erased by the grain of human ideology—

each agenda the wrong color of ego.
What color and nationality is a soul?

There's no racial control over anyone's soul—
no spatial hold, no ethnic fundamentalism.

All these centuries later, still the violence?
I stand and say, still the violence.
Yet my favorite century remains this one,
filled with the wonder of possibility.

I'm not greedy. I'm just
stubborn for righteousness.
Now, in our century, everything written
is midrash, nothing written

that is not midrashim.
We approach the unknown
by means of the known.
A world without transcendence

isn't livable.
If God is silent, if God is only silent in listening,
then, God is in my exhaling chant.
There aren't enough terrorists to kill

every voice. Then, I sing for those unable
or unwilling to sing. I sing for all of us together.
I choose the living company of hope.
Drop the weapons and hum your children to sleep.

I was born into three countries: birthright,
ethnic, and naturalized. I was born a world citizen.
I want the world. I sing for the world.
I pray for the world to sing back.

The Heart as an Inner Kingdom

Why do we always seek from without?
How even the architecture of churches
in the Western world aspire

upward to Heaven, aspire to reach that lofty height.
Yet how the Orthodox churches are designed
to hold Heaven here on earth,

the cupola resting on the walls of the world.
I take this image from architecture
and sit within myself. I take my heart

and examine my motive, my attitude.
This is all I may present to the Lord.
I give my heart as an inner kingdom.

No formalism, but form with substance.
I give the state of my heart, in which
tradition serves me but doesn't rule me.

I ask the grace of the Lord
to live in my heart,
to let me enter through my introspection.

I put an end to conversations
with the outer world.
Here is the kingdom of the world—

within this beating heart, this pulsing home,
architecture and form
enough to live in.

The Internal Psalm

Deep within me, a prayer is saying itself.
In my still depths, a psalm is intoning its rhythm
underneath what I do and say, underneath
the thought of my thought, the will of my will.
Deep within me, the chant of my father.
Low within, the heatbeat beneath my heartbeat.
The echo of my thought before my thought.
I am living in my existence. I am singing in my living.
From waking and from sleep, from a depth
I can't explain, the voice of my creation,
and the timepiece of my time. Way within,
I resonate the prayer that is a song, the song
that is a heartbeat, a blood pulse. Braided
in my breathing is borne the song of an individual
in the soul's community, the name of my father
and myself, the name of the sung Lord living within.

Thrice-Holy

In the Orthodox Church, all prayer is Trinitarian.
Even prayer teaches that God is dialogue, not monologue.
Therefore, the Son. Therefore, the Spirit. Therefore, us.

As children, we are enabled to call the Father.
We address our Father as Father, seeking to share
divine being and will, by giving our will freely.

Prayer is a dialogue of silence, carried on
in the quiet of our hearts. We lift
our mind and heart to the Lord, merely

to stand in his presence, to be constantly
aware of his presence, to remember his name.
We are to ever walk in the presence of the Lord.

Just the sound of a hush. Just the approach
of silence to lead to the approach of stillness.
Stillness.

Meet me there, gratitude for receipt
and gratitude for being, present and felt,
stillness answering back.

The Lord of Silence

Lord, speak to me of your silence.

God's silence is the indictment of my sins.

God's silence is his listening
to repentance.

God's silence is his patience
and his patience.

His is the stillness of water
in which I crane to glimpse a mirror.

His is the moment in which I pause
for breath and reflection.

Lord, speak to me of your silence.

Give me the quiet lap of your presence
that I may rest upon, to listen
in return.

Let God Speak Through the Passage of Time

A Song of the Going Up

We go into the earth, for the peace of the earth,
the seasons welling above us.

Most of us become the earth again.
And some resist the earth in a sleep of wholeness.

Their bodies intact and incorrupt through time,
riding whole through centuries, flesh and bone

remaining flesh and bone. Holy *leipsana*:
the going up that is stillness. Real evidence

that even the death of flesh can hold
living grace and spirit. That even death falls

to the incorrupt, the incorrupt body surviving still.
How the death of his saints is precious in the eyes

of the Lord. How we can exhume the evidence
of a life in God: the still-reverberating blessing

from a dead hand. The skin, intact and sanctified,
skin gone the color of rosewood and fragrant.

Even the hair on the back of the hand,
visible and insistent on the Lord.

Life extended in death, and life intact.
A way for us to witness proof we sometimes need,

to let us ponder our existence, to sing in the going up,
to let God speak to us through the passage of time.

Essence and Energy of God

Never a moment when we don't say
something to ourselves in our heads.

Where God is dialogue
and not monologue—

even in a closed room,
the air moves.

Even in stillness, stillness
moves.

Adoration

May we speak of love without a word?
May we only feel the depth and awareness
of the Lord, our reality and our dependence?
May we give our being, mouthing the word *awe,*
our only stance, stillness, our only attitude, wordless—
and nothing, nothing else can approximate.

The Psalm of Even

Even the stones of the earth
know more theology than people do.

Even the gray boulders down to the pebbles
have more to speak of the Lord,

have more insight into God and Heaven
than we humans, busy with our houses.

Even when we roll for success, we can't
break even, doing even worse by losing.

The world's understanding is smooth and even.
Even the slide of loose gravel underneath our soles

speaks more eloquently than our huffing.
Even the acid rains of our making repent

better into the frame of the earth. It's an even exchange.
Even the earth holds more theology in its grave.

Even the stones of the earth speak
more profoundly in their resting stillness.

Even the mountains bow down to their valleys.
Even the thatched villages hold their humility.

Even the wisping clouds cover their faces to Heaven.
Even we know what we're supposed to be,

though we never gave any successive generation
an even chance. Even children, who don't inherit

any stand on even ground, sense the limitations of adults.
Even children perceive the world whimpers its knowledge.

Even the globe groans to get back to the garden.
Even the parched deserts.

Even the strata of forest sedge, its diminishing girth.
Even the stones of the earth.

The Psalm of Then

Then, the Lord heard me in the wilderness of my soul.

Then, the lost place of me became clear.

Then, I recognized distraction for what it is.

Then, I was freed from the desert of diversion.

Then, I was moved to the green oasis within me.

Then, the still voice of the Lord was as the depth of water.

Then, I could cease the constant music in my head.

Then, I could move beyond myself and the noise of myself.

Then, I could hear the smallness of my own voice.

Then, the still voice of the Lord was as the depth of water.

Then, the lost place of me became clear as a cascade.

Then, I could hear the bass of my name.

Then, I heard the Lord in the wilderness of my soul.

Then, stillness and stillness and stillness sang.

In Peace Made Perfect

These trees are a peaceful place.

This tiny brook running through the village
of Meldreth, England, is a peaceful place.

The donkey Shandy in the brook's meadow
accentuates the serenity held here.

The cliff of Requa, California, above the Pacific coastline
is a peaceful place.

How these elegant redwoods are tranquil,
combing the follicled light through their cowls.

These trees
are a peaceful place.

Lord, let us take peace where we can find it. Let us cultivate
peace in the small and quiet places, the blessed places.

The trees and cascading surf of Requa Beach.
The solitude of our prayerful hands.

Lord, Father, I find peace in you
and in the natural world you made.

The green and blue hills, the lovely hills,
step and step off into distance.

The Midlands of Welford are a peaceful place.
My childhood with my father

is a hallowed place forever.
Father in Heaven, I grew peaceful

for being raised in grateful peace.
Father, I give contentment back to my children now.

I sing for all the peaceful places my soul
now wanders—the rhubarb fields of Foxton,

the era of a country village
in which peace settled

like deeply-felt breathing after a war.
Nothing human was ever perfect

but there were places in this world
that helped us come close—

the stand of trees, the silver-ribboned brook,
the villages of England, the sleeping train stations—

all pacific, all pacific I sing.
Bring it all back to memory and gratitude

for the striving, thankfulness for the breathing.
It was enough to live in peace for our time.

Only when we die are we made perfect.
The green and blue hills, the lovely hills,

step and step off into distance.
And there, we stand before the Lord,

pacific and fully present in stillness,
surrounded by forest, by meadow,

by the peace of the world.

Stillness, Stillness Seeks the Lord

A Psalm in Stillness

The world has its nuclear weapons. We have our nuclear prayer.
And prayer becomes implosion
to change the landscape of our interior.

Only the poverty of language
can give us a way to encounter and recognize
what has created us.

We are made to commune
and there is no faith without language.

The purest communication—to sit together wordlessly,
to be in each other's presence.

As my father and I sit in each other's presence,
content beyond words and still beyond movement.

In stillness, are even our thoughts still?
In stillness, are we at peace?

In stillness is where God meets us best.
In stillness can be the most intimate encounter.

I confront myself in stillness.
Lord, Father, let me truly be still and know.

Then, what is stillness

but the living presence, the living being—
in contentment, in assuredness, in stability?

What is this feeling of mystical transcendence,
prayer extending from my breath, my hands, my vision?
Nothing naïve and everything innocent.

In depth of stillness, I feel
the presence of the Lord.
I feel such assuredness that is a living calmness—

a conviction that is what it is,
a living stillness that breathes in me—through me—with me.

I feel measured divinity
even to my fingertips, the ends of my hair, the depth

of the infinite, union with all
life and the Lord of life.

In the end, there is only
a quiet kind of joy.

Oh, I drift inside the unsayable.

I can only recognize the unpronounceable—
only enough to say, I know.

Alive in the hush, aware of everything.
The motion of stillness seeking.

I drift, I drift

inside the unsayable.

Even this—